The Cool of the Wild

D1335181

The Cool of the Wild

AN EXTREMIST'S GUIDE
TO ADVENTURE SPORTS

Howard Tomb

CB

CONTEMPORARY
BOOKS

CHICAGO

Library of Congress Cataloging-in-Publication Data

Tomb, Howard, 1959–
    The cool of the wild : an extremist's guide to adventure
sports / Howard Tomb.
      p.   cm.
    ISBN 0-8092-3774-1
    1. Outdoor recreation.   2. Outdoor recreation—
Humor. I. Title.
GV191.6.T64   1994
796.5—dc20
                              94-7290
                                CIP

Copyright © 1994 by Howard Tomb
All rights reserved
Published by Contemporary Books, Inc.
Two Prudential Plaza, Chicago, Illinois 60601-6790
Manufactured in the United States of America
International Standard Book Number: 0-8092-3774-1
10   9   8   7   6   5   4   3   2   1

For Annie

Contents

The Joy of Terror

We who live in "developed" societies are up to our ears in static—seemingly random signals that make no sense. As technologies pump ever more information at us, our confusion deepens and our worries multiply like cockroaches. We become distracted from what's truly important.

Some of us are able to break out of the modern fog, however. People who survive near-fatal accidents or recover from serious illnesses, for instance, often change their priorities; they have a new appreciation for the untouchable, for the mysterious glories of life. They have a new thirst for beauty and a new distaste for all things petty, mean-spirited, and quotidian. They feel comfortable telling their bosses to suck dogmeat.

Unfortunately, postindustrial chaos overwhelms most of these survivors, and they mix up their priorities and sink back into their worrying, sniveling ways.

A few members of modern society, however, regularly refresh their courage: the wilderness adventurers, the unflappable masters, the cool of the wild. Instead of relying on luck to survive an awful disease or car crash, for example, they hone their skills in one or more dangerous pursuits so they can dance along the brink of disaster regularly and *on purpose*.

Because the cool of the wild keep their priorities straight, they can remain calm when, say, somebody drops the last piece of their favorite lasagna on a filthy kitchen floor. My lasagna has hairs on it now, they might think to themselves, but at least my skull has not been crushed by a falling block of granite.

While a postindustrial person might shout curses, endure a potentially lethal rise in blood pressure, and feed the soiled lasagna to the nearest dog, the master simply accepts the many-layered nature of lasagna, peels away the gritty portion, and enjoys the rest. I have slightly less lasagna now, the master might think, but a twenty-two-foot saltwater crocodile is not tearing my leg off.

Finding this kind of peace and poise in our frenetic world takes practice and dedication, but huge are the rewards. Grace and terror combine in a multitude of forms; this book is meant to help readers achieve them using the more popular and effective methods.

The sports are divided into four general categories: extreme climbing, extreme skiing, extreme wetness, and extreme falling. It's hard to judge which is most insane: jumping off an office building, for example, climbing a wall of ice, or sailing across the Pacific Ocean accompanied only by a small dog. Although all of these flood the bloodstream with Exotic Chemicals of Fear, different sports appeal to different kinds of people. We have provided exclusive Archetype ProFiles to guide you in exploring new avenues of terror and deciding which group of nutbags you'd like to join.

Break a leg.

Note for the Nonsportsperson

Few can master all of the sports described in this book; people without the time or money[1] to practice will never master any of them. Although nonsportspersons[2] may never walk the walk, this book will help them at least talk the talk. We have provided exclusive Suave-Matic Quick Reference Guides to proper sporting lingo.

While some readers may never hold the title of Terror Master, they will be able to stand near masters without embarrassment, understand some of what masters say, correctly fling terminology in the masters' vicinity, and appreciate how deeply suave the masters really are. Some of the masters' confidence and charm may even rub off.

---

[1] Or guts.
[2] Sissies.

Anyone willing to show respect for beauty and nature is welcome to join the masters of terror at the launch area, the base camp, and the bar. Just don't crowd them. And pay no attention to their smell.

Disclaimer

Due to (a) the deadly nature of the sports described in this book and (b) the unwise nature of millions of people who are able to read the English language, the author, agents, editor, printer, publisher, shippers, wholesalers, retailers, librarians, maintenance staff, and security guards accept no responsibility of any kind for anything, especially not intestinal parasites, severe injury, or death, and hereby recommend, cajole, and in extreme cases force readers to remain Super Glued into BarcaLoungers, La-Z-Boys, or Craft-Matic Adjustable Beds bolted to the floors of concrete bunkers for the rest of their lives and at all times remain on belay wearing approved helmets, UV- and impact-resistant eye protection, radio transponders, flotation vests, insect repellent, athletic supporters, sterile gauze, zinc oxide, multiple prophylactic devices, and parachutes.

Extreme Climbing

ARCHETYPE PROFILE: ROCK JOCK

Appearance: Tall, skinny, deeply unwashed.

Vehicle: 1970 Ford pickup.

House: 1970 Ford pickup.

Favorite Clothing: Snug T-shirt, loose-fitting drawstring pants.

Education: Almost two semesters at Wind River Community College, Lander, Wyoming.

Goal: Free climbing Mount Hooker.

Other Skill: Dishwashing.

Worst Fear: Having to work as a ranch hand.

MAKING LOVE TO GRANITE

Rock climbing is becoming more popular with people who went to Club Med in the 1980s. Bored by luxury and comfort, they now want to strap colorful harnesses tightly around their loins, suffer exquisitely, and have multiple achievements.

Climbers can display wealth and taste in the parking area: dozens of bits of protection at $50 each, new ropes and outfits, satin chalk bags, $300 sunglasses, whatever. Once they get on a cliff, however, they generally move out of sight, and all showing off comes to an end. Most routes are out of sight even to people holding the ropes. This makes rock climbing the ideal antiglamour sport for the nineties. Unobtrusive and inward-turning, it's existential tag-team wrestling: Your Mind, Your Body, and the Rock versus Fear, Gravity, and Irreversible Spinal Injury.

Top-Roping

The first thing climbers learn is how to get their bodies up the rock. They should start a few feet off the ground—"boulder"—for a while to learn how the shoes stick. Some climbers actually prefer bouldering because their rippling muscles and elegant techniques are more clearly visible to spectators.

Most rock climbers eventually graduate to top-roping. The climber is belayed[3] by someone holding the rope at the top of the climb, or the rope passes through a ring at the top to a belayer standing

---

[3]From the French verb meaning "to crane one's neck and become extremely bored."

below. The rope is thus always taut, and the climber will never fall more than a foot or two, so long as the belayer is not too focused on tanning or elaborate sexual fantasies.

On top-rope, climbers learn to trust the rope and the person on belay. They can concentrate on being deliberate and catlike without thinking much about paraplegia. They mix gravity with granite and come to appreciate the finer features of a cliff face, including subtle textures, hollows, hidden cracks, nubbins, six-inch centipedes, and hornets' nests.

Lead Climbing

Even the most talented climbers boulder and top-rope to hone their balance, flexibility, and strength. But there comes a time when that talent must be tested.

The earliest climbers in Europe tied handmade ropes around their waists and held the ropes in cracks with chock stones. They are now dead.

Today the principle of lead climbing is the same, except stones have been replaced by metal nuts and chocks slung with rope, webbing, or wire. Camming devices, such as Friends and Camalots, serve the same purpose with more flexibility and at much greater expense.

To lead or "free climb,"[4] a climber must learn

---

[4] People reveal their ignorance of the sport by misusing the term *free climbing*. It doesn't mean going unroped but only that the climber is clinging to the rock itself rather than artificial equipment and using the rope only to stop a fall. The word *free* distinguishes this type of climbing from aid climbing, discussed later.

the arcane craft of protection: attaching rings, called *carabiners,* to the cliff with nuts, chocks, stoppers, and so on. The rope, attached to the climber, slides through the carabiners. The belayer sits or stands below, keeping slack out of the rope, ready to hold it tight in the event of a fall.

Leaders thus fall as far past the last piece of protection as they were above it when they lost their grip. From fifteen feet above their last piece of protection, for example, they would fall thirty feet plus the stretch of the rope, another four or five feet.

Each piece of protection, including slings and carabiners, can hold five thousand pounds or so, about double the force a climber would generate in a typical leader fall. Ropes, slings, carabiners, and other pieces of protection almost never break. Climbers get killed in other ways:

- The protection wiggles out of a crack as the leader climbs above it or gets wrenched out as the leader falls past it.

- Carabiners, twisted around in a fall, open their gates and let loose the rope.

- The belayer, having drifted away in a daydream, fails to hold the rope tightly enough.

- The falling leader hits a horizontal surface before the rope runs out.

The first three errors are avoided by skilled and scrupulous lead climbers. They place protection so it won't come out while climbing or during a fall. They know how to orient their carabiners and how to recognize unreliable partners.

The possibility of error four (also known as Heavy D, Vapor-Lock, Big Dirt Nap, etc.) forces a climber to concentrate. The most challenging rock climbs have long run-outs—sections of just the right blankness where climbing is still possible but protection isn't. On a long run-out, skills perfected at ground level disappear because of the T-factor.

The T-Factor

Terror may be psychological, but it does a number on your physical body. When your legs start to shake, for example, your footing becomes less secure, and that scares you more. Your hands start to sweat so hard the rock feels slimy. You sense not only that you may peel off the rock but that your sense that you may peel off the rock may actually cause you to peel off the rock.

At this point you turn a mental corner and ask yourself the age-old Adventurer's Question: Why am I here?

Corollaries then spring to mind: (a) Is it really so bad to drink an entire six-pack of beer in a prone position while watching people fish for bass on TV? (b) Is there a God? (c) Might I make a bargain with Him right this second to save my sorry ass just this one time?

Many things can sharpen the T-factor on a rock climb. Height, for example. Any fall onto jagged boulders from over seventy feet is going to be fatal, but the deepest fears are unreasoning fears: most people find seven hundred feet scarier than seventy.

The height above the last protection or lack of confidence in its placement can make a relatively easy move seem impossible.

A climb's reputation can make it more difficult. If you've fallen from it before or it's never been climbed, it may be especially daunting.

Simple tasks can be turned into challenges by countless things: fatigue, a comment your accountant made last week, a really large spider staring at you from a crack, and so on.

We can learn to overcome the T-factor, to accept the fear and work through it, and to forget how it felt so we can put ourselves in new and even more terrifying situations next weekend.

That, in fact, is how bravery is made: practice. The happiest and most successful people have learned to swallow doubt and fear and *make the move*.

People who never exercise their courage get a flabby pluck. When they suddenly need strength to stand up to a human or spiritual enemy, they are easily beaten.

In the chart on the following page, the letters *a* through *d* can be added to a rating to make especially fine distinctions. Climbing a 5.13b route, for example, is easier than climbing a 5.13c, just as leaping over tall buildings in a single bound is easier than jumping over the moon.

THE ROCK-CLIMBING GRADING SYSTEM

Free climbs, all "grade 5," were originally rated on a scale of .1 through .9. Climbing skills and equipment surpassed the expectations of the people who devised the system, however, so the scale now goes well beyond .9. While ratings are, in the end, subjective, climbers agree on the following guidelines:

Grade 1: Walking

Grade 2: Walking uphill

Grade 3: Walking up a steep hill

Grade 4: Scrambling over things up a steep hill

Grade 5: Wanting to think about a rope

5.1: Difficult without legs

5.2: Difficult on crutches

5.3: Difficult in high heels

5.4: Difficult if more than fifty pounds overweight

5.5: Difficult if clumsy, timid, or unusually short

5.6: Difficult on first day of climbing

5.7: Difficult without basic skills and some audacity

5.8: Difficult without imagination and regular practice

Continued

THE ROCK-CLIMBING GRADING SYSTEM

(continued)

5.9: Difficult without strength
and talent

5.10: Difficult without strength,
talent, and grace

5.11: Difficult without exceptional
strength, talent, and grace

5.12: Difficult without exceptional
strength, talent, grace, and
dedication

5.13: Difficult without generous gifts
from God

5.14: Difficult without generous gifts
from Satan

Aid Climbing

Some mighty walls are too blank to hang on to. They must be aid-climbed. Yosemite has the best-known cliffs of this kind, some three thousand feet tall and often requiring days of climbing.

Aid climbers do things that would cost a free climber huge style points: they hang on to their protection and sometimes drill steel bolts into the rock, permanently scarring it.

Aid climbing is often more brutish than graceful. No wall is so blank that certain tools won't stick to it—aid climbers can drill bolts even into overhangs. As civilization advances, bolts will become more and more politically incorrect.

Equipment and Care

Use a climbing rope. Do not use a caving, rappelling, or "static" rope because it won't stretch. Hitting the end of it will remind you of hitting the ground in the fraction of a second it takes to break your body in half.

Gristleheads have been known to tow cars with climbing ropes, taking out the spring and rendering them deadly in a leader fall. Never lead on a rope if you don't know its history or if its owner is the sort of person who relies more on faith than on prudence (see "The Perils of Faith," later in this chapter).

Never step on a rope. Sharp particles, ground in, may cut through internal fibers.

Do not leave a rope in the sun for any longer than necessary, especially not in a car on a hot day. Heat and sunlight degrade the plastic fibers.

CLIMBING FINESSE

Women are among the world's best rock climbers. Focusing on flexibility, balance, and leg strength and relying less on chin-ups and other brute-force power-up methods, women are naturally better climbers.

Anyone learning to climb should follow the example of the great women climbers; testosterone and finesse are antithetical. Legs are stronger than arms—you can stand on legs all day. A lean, gymnastic woman can outclimb Sly Stallone any day of the week.

SUAVE-MATIC QUICK REFERENCE GUIDE: ROCK TALK

STATEMENT	MEANING
We had both taken twenty-foot whippers trying to free Pyrotechnics, this nasty 5.12d route on Fire Wall at the Needles.	We had both taken twenty-foot falls trying to free climb an almost completely blank face in California's southern Sierra.
Suddenly this sixteen-year-old honemaster Brit shows up and decides to try an on-sight red-point—with a partial set of stoppers and two Camalots.	A mere child from a place where they don't even have big granite faces decides to free climb the route on his first attempt—without adequate protection.
He couldn't protect the crux without a #2 Tri-Cam but snagged it with a dyno move onto a thumb jam.	Despite the possibility of a long fall, he made an all-or-nothing leap and caught most of his weight with his thumb joint.
Turns out he'd already flashed Sea of Tranquility, Iceberg, and Titanic that morning, to warm up for the "hard climbs."	We thought we were witnessing a once-in-a-lifetime magic act, but the kid was just getting warmed up.

STATEMENT	MEANING
When he came down, I asked him about the dyno move, and he said he was "bloody wigged."	Not only is the little bastard better now than I'll ever be even if I quit my job to climb full-time, he's also modest enough to admit he was afraid.
I'm about to kneel down to kiss the kid's Five Ten Razors and ask for his blessing when he literally runs off to get on Pyromania, a 5.13a flake-up.	Although I was prepared to kiss his smelly shoes and worship the child as a god, he wasn't interested in disciples. He wanted to climb.

Protection. The slings and ropes used on pieces of protection get worn out even faster than climbing ropes. They should be replaced after they've absorbed a leader fall.

The Most Painful Footwear on Earth. Climbing shoes are worn a size or two too small. They are meant to turn feet into hooves. Walking in them is often such torture that some rock climbers carry sneakers or sandals[5] to walk down in. Still, nothing can replace a good pair of rock shoes.

In choosing a pair for yourself, consider how they'll be used and how much pain you're willing to endure. Novices should get a relatively comfortable, relatively stiff, relatively inexpensive all-around high-top shoe.

Grizzled vets who plan to assault major faces

ROCK-CLIMBING STYLE CHART

How climbers move is nearly as important as *whether* they do. As in all of life's pursuits, grace is fundamental to glory.

Using a 10-point gymnastic model, this style chart helps climbers keep score on each other and themselves.

Style-Point Deductions

Curse pertaining to bodily functions	−.10
Curse pertaining to the Lord	−.25
Curse pertaining to the Lord's bodily functions	−.50
Call for tension	−.20
Scream for tension	−.50

[5]Supermod sandals, such as Tevas, are lightweight but have two main disadvantages: (1) they are ultrastylish, and (2) they allow you to stub your toes severely every few minutes.

Unintelligible scream	−.90
Scream audible for more than half a mile	−1.50
Use of knee or elbow	−.40
Use of chin	−.50
Skull jam	−.75
Gonad jam	−.90
Use of protection as handhold or foothold	−1.00
Touching tree or bush with hand or foot	−1.00
Biting tree or bush	−1.20
Loss of nut, chock, or stopper in crack	−.75
Loss of Friend or Camalot in crack	−1.00
Loss of shoe in crack	−1.50
Body part stuck in crack	−2.00
Causing pebble to fall	−.05
Causing rock to fall	−.35
Causing boulder to fall	−1.25
Fart audible to belayer	−.10
Sex organ visible to belayer	−1.50
Whining	−2.00
Color-coordinated outfit	−3.00
Bolt placement	−10.00

THE PERILS OF FAITH: JUDGING A CLIMBING PARTNER

Hanging by our fingernails on a cliff, with a single rope as a lifeline, we all appreciate the possibility of injury or death. *Holding* a rope while someone *else* is hanging on to a cliff, some people are able to forget about the terrible possibilities.

These people make poor climbing partners. They should be left behind whenever possible, preferably by the side of a remote highway at night without any money or food.

Identifying these people is simple once you understand their different mind-set. Listen for comments that reveal dangerous excesses of faith or shortages of logic:

GOOD PARTNER	BAD PARTNER
"These slings look like antiques."	"They're fine. I've fallen on them a hundred times."
"I prefer to set up a belay anchor with double opposing carabiners."	"What happens happens."
"He got off route and fell forty feet."	"The Lord decided it was his time."
"She tried to climb two grades past her ability."	"Her karma caught up with her."

GOOD PARTNER	BAD PARTNER
"Let's wear helmets."	"Trust in Jesus."
"The Lord helps those who help themselves."	"Let's rappel off this shrub."

won't be happy with a shoe until it turns their toes black and blue and makes their toenails fall off.

The two main uses for rock shoes, edging and friction, are at odds with each other in shoe design. Edging requires a sharp, stiff edge; friction requires a softer, stickier touch. By the time you're good enough to prefer one or the other, you'll probably need more than one pair of shoes.

Climbing in the Desert

Some of the best climbing is found in arid places. To survive comfortably in such a hostile environment, you should change your habits to adapt to its alien cycles.

Scalding days and frigid nights have given many desert plants and animals bad attitudes. Armed with barbs, stingers, and fangs, any one of them can turn a camping trip into a race for the emergency room.

Gila monsters are the least of your problems. To provoke a Gila you'd have to do something like stick pins in its eyes and read aloud from the latest Carlos Castaneda book. Then, to get a fatal dose of venom, you'd have to let the lizard chew on your face for about half an hour.

Rattlesnakes move faster—like shotgun blasts. They blend in so perfectly with their surroundings they need rattles to keep you from stepping on them.

Rattlesnake venom is essentially concentrated digestive juice. As it digests your muscles and bones, it makes the bite area swell up like a black, pus-filled cantaloupe from hell. The antidote is equally disagreeable, but neither is likely to kill you.

And if you don't look under rocks, you're unlikely to encounter rattlers during the day. No one except Mr. Completely Suave Person, such as a shaman, walks in the desert at night.

Unlike snakes, scorpions will come looking for you. They want to try on everybody's shoes and underwear. They've always wanted tents and sleeping bags of their very own.

A mild scorpion sting will make you wish your parents had died at birth. A serious sting, from a Central American or African scorpion, for example, can cause blindness, psychosis, coma, and death in minutes. Compared to a bad scorpion sting, multiple tarantula bites would seem like a weekend in Aspen.

Avoiding contact with prickly flora and fauna of the desert is easy—keep your vehicle in gear and the windows rolled up.

Seek shelter from the sun. Move slowly and only during the early morning and late afternoon. Leave the night to creatures who have spent at least eighty million years evolving to survive in it.

If you must ingest mind-altering substances, have one member of your party remain sober enough to contradict the desert's spectral beings, who are every bit as dangerous as those made of flesh and blood.

VERTICAL ICE:
PLEASURE, PAIN, AND MENTAL HEALTH

ARCHETYPE PROFILE:
ACE ICE CLIMBER

Appearance: Calm, alert, malnourished.
Home: Ouray, Colorado.
House: Mobile home.
Decor: Mountaineering posters, battered climbing equipment, wet socks and mittens.
Favorite Clothing: North Face.
Goal: Everest summit.
Current Reading: *Journal of the American Alpine Club: Accidents in American Mountaineering,* 1984.
Worst Fear: Not being invited to join the summit team.

Climbing ice as a novice isn't much like rock climbing; it's more like falling *through* ice on a frozen lake: one gets intensely cold and wet while cursing and flailing in wild-eyed terror as Death begins the backswing of his ragged scythe.

Masterful ice climbing, on the other hand, resembles vertical ballet in wool accompanied by vicious-looking serrated steel tools.

First developed by European climbers to cross glaciers, ice climbing is now a sport in its own right. Glacial snow is usually too even and yielding to offer a real challenge, so most ice climbing today is performed on (partly) frozen waterfalls. Structural irregularities and varying degrees of hardness can make water ice respond to blows by exploding in a climber's face or peeling away in blocks the size of upright pianos.

The two basic levels of ice climbing parallel those of rock climbing: top-roping and leading.

Top-Roping on Ice

A beginner wears a harness tied to the end of a rope, which passes through a metal ring tied to a tree at the top of the climb and back down to a person on belay,[6] who takes up slack as the climber ascends and holds the rope taut when the climber falls, preventing a drop of more than one or two feet if the rope and the mittens holding it aren't covered in ice and extremely slippery.

Top-roping is almost perfectly safe unless the climber cuts his or her rope with his or her freshly sharpened serrated steel axes. The belayer faces more danger: falling ice pianos. The belayer takes cover or stands well off to one side while wearing an

---

[6]From the French verb meaning "to stand around and freeze your butt off."

officially approved helmet and an alert expression.

The beginner hammers furiously, trying to bury nine inches of axe into the ice, and then discovers the ice, only four inches thick, covers a running waterfall. Ice water shoots from the hole as if from a hose onto the climber, usually down his or her neck.

As the hammering and cursing become more vivid and high-pitched, the climber bangs entire sets of knuckles on the solid ice. After putting enough effort into each blow, the climber will eventually notice blood seeping out through the mittens and staining the ice. Flying ice chips will cut the climber's face, providing an extra dash of machismo to the climber's appearance.

But hammering the ice is not enough. The climber also bangs away with the front points of the crampons, kicking blocks down to flatten helpless winter creatures such as belayers and bruising the climber's knees and shins right into the bone.

Civilians who witness such a display may suggest the climber be immediately committed to a locked psychiatric ward. Experienced climbers know the novice who does not give up trying to master such a painful and ridiculous sport may have a future in winter mountaineering, perhaps even as a lead climber on ice.

Lead Climbing: No Holiday on Ice

A lead ice climber's harness remains attached to the rope, but the rope does not pass through a ring at the top of the climb. Instead it passes through rings, called carabiners, *below* the climber, which are attached to ice screws, and finally into the ice-covered mittens of the belayer.

A leader fall therefore continues past the last ice screw and stops only when the slack comes out of the rope. As with lead climbing on rock, if the last screw were ten feet below the climber, for example, the fall would continue for twenty feet plus the stretch in the rope—probably another four or five feet—for a total drop of about twenty-five feet.

This calculation assumes the last ice screw stays in the ice, but that is known as a "wild-ass" assumption. When you twist six- or nine-inch metal screws into ice, its propensity for shattering is heightened. A moderate fall can easily transfer two thousand pounds of force to the "pro"—the protection, in this case the ice screw—making it want to break out of the ice very, very much.

Rock climbers can sometimes take leader falls on sheer cliffs without serious injury. Granite holds "pro" more reliably than ice does. Rock climbers often hit the end of the rope before they hit a horizontal surface.

Few walls of ice are sheer—they almost invariably get wider toward the bottom. Thus a leader fall on ice almost invariably involves ice buttresses before it involves the taut end of the rope. Later the climber's many steel blades must be removed by surgeons at the nearest hospital or by pathologists at the nearest medical examiner's office.

Thus we arrive at an important conclusion: *Lead ice climbers must never, ever fall.* If you wait until you're fifty feet up a waterfall before you come to this conclusion, you might become alarmed and lose your concentration.

The top of an ice climb, the highest point from the ground, almost always has the thinnest ice, if any. Luckily for climbers who are trying only to save their lives and have given up on style points, ice axes easily and solidly penetrate the trees found near the top of many waterfalls. Axes also penetrate the mud and gravel of the top of a waterfall, but they have less structural integrity than living pine trees.

Once you understand how berserk it is to lead ice, you can enjoy watching someone else do it. Master ice climbers might remind you of Joe Namath or Mike Baryshnikov—they don't seem to be *trying* very hard. There isn't a lot of fuss. The blade of the hammer goes an inch deep, just far enough to hold the climber's weight plus about four ounces. The climb is fluid; each motion is made with a definite purpose. Each step sticks.

Like other superb athletes and artists, master ice climbers can make you imagine for a moment that you could do what they do and be as cool as they are.

Regular Crampons vs. Foot Fangs

Foot Fangs are not ideal for hiking to the climb because they're heavier, narrower, and thicker than regular crampons. Foot Fangs have twice as many points in front, however, so they provide a better grip when toe-pointing on a vertical ice climb.

Their highly boss name makes Foot Fangs

worth the extra price to some people. You'll hear them saying things like "Give me some tension unless you want a mouthful of Foot Fangs" or "This stewardess takes one look at my Foot Fangs and goes, 'You'll have to check those, sir.' Like I'm going to hijack a plane with aluminum footwear. Like, 'Listen up, people! This plane is going to Mont Blanc, or I chop this chick's toes off with my Foot Fangs!' "

ICE-CLIMBING SOUND EFFECTS

EXPERT	NOVICE
"Snickt. Snickt. Snickt. Snickt. Snickt. Snickt."	"Thuhchnk THuh-HUHTCHHHHnkaKK thuhCHNKAthUH-chaCkshit! CHUK-CHUKCHUK-THKAKK Ow!"

Suave-Matic Equipment Note: Gaiters

Crampons tend to tear the hell out of $250 North Face pants. Hanging shreds of Gore-Tex might make you look like you spent a hard day at the office, but pros are able to go home with pants intact for two reasons: (1) they place their crampons carefully and with a sense of purpose, and (2) they wear snug gaiters to help prevent snagging.

The snuggest and best gaiters are old-fashioned lace-up jobs you can't buy anywhere. They have to be custom-made. Contrary to popular opinion, *sewing is suave*, especially when the seamstress or seamster is able to throw together Gore-Tex outerwear.

How to Sharpen the Twenty-Eight Hardened Steel Blades You Will Need

Sharp tools are essential to graceful ice climbing because they penetrate ice when wielded gently. Dull blades, because they tend to shatter the ice, lead to repeated flailing at the same spot, which eventually leaves the climber with nothing but rock and waterfall beneath.

Using a flat metal file, bring the blades of your axes and crampons to knife-edge sharpness with smooth, steady motions, at a consistent angle, away from the direction of the points. Once the blades are sharp enough to carve ripe tomatoes, dull the edges with one or two light strokes of the file. This will help prevent microscopic bending of the edges during use and will make the tools slightly less hazardous to clothing and flesh.

BAD ALTITUDE

Arctic Comfort

Once you've mastered ice climbing, you're ready to assault a major peak's not-so-tender anatomy. All major peaks are shrouded in arctic weather during

---

ARCHETYPE PROFILE: ACE MOUNTAINEER

Appearance: Hard, weathered, well-groomed, smart.

Home: Seattle.

House: Four-bedroom custom-built log cabin with indoor pool.

Education: Master's degree in engineering.

Employment: Owner of successful software companies, brew pubs, and espresso bars.

Vehicles: BMW M1, Land Rover.

Worst Fear: Turning own kids into orphans.

---

the summer.[7] Traveling in an environment so cold it is nearly sterile has its rewards: profound solitude, wind chills below −100° F, and plenty of free ice.

Penguins, polar bears, seals, and some rugged species of lichen can live comfortably in arctic conditions at sea level. In arctic conditions above fourteen thousand feet, all living creatures need special gear, such as sleeping bags, and special techniques, such as igloo-building skills.

A well-made snow cave or igloo is a relatively warm 32° F inside, quiet, and roomy. It will stand up

---

[7]In winter, the weather becomes Martian.

to any wind on the planet. A tent, flapping in a gale, is louder inside than a speeding A-train. Heavy snow can crush any tent and all hopes of survival.

No book could replace skilled mountain guides or teachers, but here are some tips for staying comfortable on big mountains.

Igloo Construction. Using the snow saw you so wisely brought along, remove blocks of the firmest snow you can easily cut from a circular hole four or five feet deep and at least eight feet across. Ring the hole with the blocks cut from it. Ideal bricks for an igloo base measure about two feet long and a foot wide and tall. Steadily smaller blocks complete rings around the hole, slightly tapered to form a dome with a ventilation hole at the peak.

The entrance should lead down from surface level and back up into the igloo, to trap heat inside. After a day or two, the inside of the igloo will harden from your warmth. Sprinkling water on the outside will harden it further, until it's nearly hard enough to climb on. A sheet of clear ice can be used as a window to play peekaboo with polar bears.

Snow Cave Construction. A sturdy shovel and a large drift of firm snow are required for a snow cave. Dig an L-shaped entrance into the drift and up into the cave. If possible, dig the cave at least high enough to stand up in while hunched. Dig a shelf for each person to sleep on, because your body heat will cause the walls to sweat and may lead to the formation of a puddle in the lowest area of the cave. A small hole in the roof will help prevent asphyxiation, allow some moist air to escape, and keep things as dry as possible[8] inside the cave.

Clothing. Like shelters, clothing must be carefully chosen if it is supposed to be warm when covered with ice. Icy leather, for example, can't keep feet warm. Boots must be kept from the elements with polar bear fur or heavy plastic. Losing even three or four toes will make your gait look goofy for the rest of your life, not that you can expect to live very long with gangrene in a blinding snowstorm.

Arctic mittens come in sets: two or more pairs made from synthetic or real wool and breathable shells of arctic animal skins or nylon. In truly cold places, leather gloves are nothing but a bad joke.

Clothing is also worn in layers of wool, which wicks moisture away from the body, and covered by a heavy fur or nylon coat. An arctic jacket has a seriously insulated hood to protect the hat. Fur fringe around the hood protects the face from wind and frostbite. People who lose their noses and ears to frostbite frequently experience a dramatic decline in their dating opportunities.

The serious problem of dehydration must be fended off constantly. Getting water in arctic environments means melting snow, and that means carrying plenty of fuel. Firewood is as scarce in the arctic as string bikinis.

Wise campers spend the night with hot bottles of water in their sleeping bags and thus wake up with liquid for drinking, cooking, brushing teeth, etc.

---

[8]Which is pretty damn damp.

Any expert can answer this question: Anthropologists believe natives of the arctic circle developed the first sunglasses because they wanted to (a) look more like Jack Lord, (b) prevent snow blindness, or (c) keep their eyeballs warm?

The answer is (d) all of the above. The Inuit developed bone "sunglasses" with thin slits to let light in. Fashion issues aside, these were necessary to survival because sunlight on snow can be literally blinding after just a few hours of exposure. When snow blindness kicks in, your eyeballs feel like they're filled with sand. You may not be able to open your eyes for days.

The blindness may go away after a day or two in the dark, but night vision can be impaired permanently. Even one day of blindness in polar bear country is hazardous, and people who spend six months of every year in the dark need their night vision.

Experts, on the snow in daylight, wear expensive sunglasses at least some of the time. People hoping to be mistaken for experts may wear expensive sunglasses in bars. The best sunglasses fit snugly against the wearer's face, firmly grip the wearer's head, and block at least 95 percent of ultraviolet rays.

Altitude Sickness

Many major mountain climbs, including Everest's simpler routes, require no unusual technical skill—they're difficult primarily because the air is thin. Otherwise these climbs would be nothing but long walks over crevasse-filled glaciers and avalanche-prone snowfields in horrific frigid weather.

The insidious effects of altitude exaggerate many mountaineering hazards. Hiking up a mountain is tiring enough, but deep sleep can be impossible in thin air. Climbers become more exhausted with each passing day and begin to snap at each other.

Mild altitude sickness causes nausea. Loss of appetite makes climbers weaker still and more susceptible to the cold. Severe exhaustion and lack of food can lead to errors in judgment. Bitter arguments erupt over things like who sleeps in the middle and whose breath smells more like Calcutta in July.

Despite the dryness of the environment, climbers may be too nauseated to drink enough water. With advanced altitude sickness they may not even be able to hold water down. Their tans fade to an olive drab color, and they may experience crying jags.

Fluid in the lungs can cause severe coughing fits, making sleep more difficult for everyone. In later stages of the sickness, fluid can suddenly swell key organs like hearts and brains in pulmonary or cerebral edema. Cardiac arrest, coma, and death tend to dampen vacation spirits.

A slow ascent allows bodies to acclimate and prevents altitude sickness in most people. Hanging around in a tent or even an igloo for a week gets deeply boring, however. Some climbers speed their acclimation by reducing the fluids in their bodies; they take prescription diuretics and drink as little liquid as possible. Some pansies still carry bottled oxygen.

Once altitude sickness kicks in, the only certain cure is descent. Fierce mountain weather can make evacuation impossible, however. Scientists have developed a blow-up recompression chamber called a Gamow bag, and they want about two thousand bucks for it.

High-altitude mountaineering has many risks; each climber must decide when they outweigh the potential satisfaction of reaching the summit. As a general rule, however, twenty-four consecutive hours of violent barfing signal the end of someone's climb.

How to Carry 150 Pounds

Reaching summits over twenty thousand feet usually requires more food, fuel, and equipment than climbers can carry. They have four options:

1. Drag some of the load on sleds.
2. Make two trips with more than seventy-five pounds on each.
3. Hire porters or beasts of burden.
4. Try a different sport, like alpine climbing or lawn darts.

A plastic sled allows a climber to drag more than a hundred pounds across relatively smooth snowfields. A drag bag made of heavy plastic is less durable and less slippery but doesn't have the flipping problems of a sled, which can cause fits of howling and cursing.

The brute-force method of carrying half a load at a time is still favored by expeditions where sleds are impractical—below the snow line, for instance—and where minimum wage laws are in effect.

Jet-set adventurers find most of the world's biggest mountains in regions where hard currency is still something of a novelty. The local people and their animals will cheerfully carry essential gear deep into the wilderness, where they will suddenly stop and renegotiate their contracts, putting a jet-set vacation in jeopardy. This will cause the vacationers to curse and stamp the ground with their $400 hiking boots.

Third World porters don't accept out-of-continent checks, Visa, *or* American Express. They want cash or Gore-Tex. Experienced expedition leaders are always prepared to have all their fancy gear held hostage by short, stocky guys who do not respond to threats of legal action.

The final alternative—taking up a different sport—rules out the unique satisfaction of climbing big mountains unless you're one of those utterly fearless ur-mountaineer demigods known as alpine climbers. Those who reach major summits using alpine technique[9] are admired by dozens of people around the world.

Mountain guerrillas, alpine climbers travel in small groups without enough food, fuel, or gear to mount a proper siege. They cannot afford to wait for perfect weather or hang around reading Norman

---

[9]And survive.

SUAVE-MATIC QUICK REFERENCE GUIDE: HIMALAYA SPEAK

STATEMENT	MEANING
High camp was brisk on Chomolungma.	We were pinned down by Verdun-like weather 26,000 feet up Mount Everest.
Three days of wind.	Huddled in a tent in 120-mph winds, we didn't eat, sleep, or breathe for seventy-two hours.
I got disoriented as I started back to base camp.	Trying to get help for my friends who were dying of cerebral edema, I got lost in the whiteout.
I took an unexpected glissade.	I fell three thousand feet into Tibet.
My left leg got pretty tough on the hike out.	My 180-mile hop to the road with my right leg broken in four places was an epic.

McLean until they acclimate. They go straight for the top on what sometimes become suicide missions.

An alpine ascent of a major peak takes more than skill, luck, audacity, and good weather; it also takes rare physical gifts that cannot be acquired with any known workout regimen. The fact that some people can perform athletic feats at altitudes where mere mortals have already slipped into comas is still something of a mystery to scientists. After decades of careful study they have determined

MOUNT EVEREST BY ANY OTHER NAME

In 1863 Andrew Waugh, director of the Indian Survey Office, named what had just been proved to be the world's tallest peak in honor of his predecessor, George "Mount" Everest.

Oddly, the people who live in Nepal and Tibet, where the mountain is located, already had names for the mountain and continue to use them to this day. Learn the names to avoid getting trapped in your narrow, Western view of reality.

COUNTRY	NAME	TRANSLATION
Nepal	Sagarmatha	Godhead
Tibet	Chomo-lungma	Mother of the World
China	Jolmo Lungma	Triumph of Communism

NAME-DROPPER'S NOTE

Tibet's Melungtse, at 23,560 feet, is not a tall mountain by Himalayan standards, but it is one of the most difficult climbs because every side is not only extremely steep but also sheathed in ice. The mountain catches high winds and hellish weather roughly 365 days a year.

China invaded Tibet in 1959, forcing the Dalai Lama, a super guy and the nation's spiritual leader, into exile. Many native Tibetans yearn for independence and would appreciate your support. Many Chinese, on the other hand, are understandably sensitive about this matter and would rather you didn't mention it. The men who run China say the occupation is "an internal affair." Luckily the bloodthirsty bastards will soon die of old age and go straight to the blackest, hottest, slimiest depths of hell.

that having Sherpas or Incas among your ancestors is a distinct advantage.

Pioneering a new alpine route on a major peak does not carry the cachet of, say, setting a Rose Bowl record for rushing yardage. Mountaineering success almost never leads to significant product endorsement contracts or more attractive sex partners. That gives high-altitude mountaineering its special purity as a sport—the summit must be its own reward.

Surfing the Alps

Snow avalanches occur when layers of snow have different consistencies and don't stick together well. A minuscule change in temperature, a plane high above, a puff of wind, or a passing bonehead can unstick a layer and cause a slide. A small slide can pin bodies beneath the snow and deprive them of air. A medium-size slide can rip large trees out at the roots, punch cars off roads, and flatten houses.

Slides of rock and ice are worse.

We can avoid avalanches by staying off steep, unstable slopes. When we must climb such slopes, we minimize exposure by staying as far to one side of the slope as possible and wearing climbing helmets.

When we're forced to cross avalanche-prone slopes, we wear radio transponders and generally rope up. If we are on skis, we might wear long leashes that a search party can follow to our bodies.

When we start an avalanche, we scream horrifying warnings to all living creatures below us.

Given a choice between the two methods of surviving a slide, ducking beats riding. A boulder or a big flake of rock can serve as an umbrella to deflect the mighty freight train of an avalanche.

Such shelter is rarely available on snowfields, of course. Before belaying from an exposed position on an unstable snowfield, we would be wise to dig a hole big enough to duck into and deep enough to get under the layers that might slide.

In the absence of shelter we must ride the slide. Whether it is made of snow, ice, rocks, trees, cars, houses, elk, or some blend of these elements, our technique is the same: we use skiing and swimming motions to stay on top of the wave. Bodysurfing a wall of rolling boulders is no Florida vacation, but we might as well try it if the alternative is becoming part of the geology.

If we are drawn under snow, we do not struggle; we cup our hands over our mouths in a futile attempt to leave a breathing space when the wave comes to a stop. We do not waste our breath with screams for help because the snow will muffle them.

If we come out on top, we immediately look for anyone who got buried, using the radio transponders we turned on before the avalanche. Without transponders, of course, we would be forced to use our telescoping avalanche probes to poke the snow for our companions before they suffocated.

Probing a snowfield for bodies is inefficient and unlikely to save anybody's life. When friends and relatives of the suffocated asked why we tried to cross an unstable snowfield without radio transponders, we would have only one answer: "We are brainless amateurs who deserve to be locked in a federal penitentiary with Mike Tyson for the rest of our natural lives."

FINE POINTS OF
EXPEDITION BEHAVIOR

A good expedition team is like a powerful, well-oiled, finely tuned marriage. Members cook together, carry burdens together, face challenges together, and finally go to bed together.

A bad expedition, on the other hand, is an awkward, ugly, embarrassing thing characterized by bickering, filth, frustration, and crunchy macaroni.

Nearly all bad expeditions have one thing in common: poor expedition behavior (EB). This is true even if team members follow the stated rules.[10]

Unfortunately, too many rules of expedition behavior remain unspoken. Some leaders seem to assume that their team members have strong and generous characters like their own. But many would-be woodspeople need more rules spelled out. Here are ten of them.

RULE NO. 1:
GET THE HELL OUT OF BED.

Suppose your tentmates get up early to fetch water and fire up the stove while you lie comatose in your sleeping bag. As they run an extensive equipment check, coil ropes, and fix your breakfast, they hear you begin to snore.

Last night you were their buddy; now they're drawing up a list of things about you that make them want to spit. They will devise cruel punishments for you. You deserve them.

---

[10]Such as Don't Step on the Rope, Separate Kerosene and Food, No Soap in the River, No Raccoons in the Tent, Keep Your Ice Axe Out of My Eye, etc.

RULE NO. 2: DO NOT BE CHEERFUL BEFORE BREAKFAST.

Some people wake up as happy and perky as fluffy bunny rabbits. They put stress on those who wake up as mean as rabid wolverines.

Exhortations such as "Rise and shine, sugar!" and "Greet the dawn, pumpkin!" have been known to provoke pungent expletives from wolverine types. These curses, in turn, may offend bunny rabbit types. Indeed they are issued with the intent to offend. Thus the day begins with flying fur and hurt feelings.

The best early-morning EB is simple: be quiet.

RULE NO. 3: DO NOT COMPLAIN. ABOUT ANYTHING. EVER.

Visibility is four inches, it's −10° F, and wind-driven hailstones are embedding themselves in your face like shotgun pellets. Must you mention it? Do you think your friends haven't noticed the weather? Make a suggestion. Tell a joke. Lead a prayer. Do not lodge a complaint.

Yes, your pack weighs eighty-seven pounds and your cheap backpack straps are actually cutting into your flesh. Were you promised a personal Sherpa? Did someone cheat you out of a mule team? If you can't carry your weight, get a motor home.

RULE NO. 4: LEARN TO COOK AT LEAST ONE THING WELL.

One expedition trick is so old it is no longer amusing: on the first cooking assignment the clever "chef" prepares a dish that resembles, say, Sock du Sweat en Sauce de Waste Toxique. The cook hopes to be permanently relieved of cooking duties.

This is a childish approach to a problem that's been with us since people first started throwing lizards on the fire. Tricks are not in the team spirit. If you don't like to cook, offer to wash dishes and prepare the one thing you do know how to cook. Even if it's only tea.

Remember: talented camp cooks sometimes get invited to join major Himalayan expeditions, all expenses paid.

RULE NO. 5: EITHER SHAMPOO OR DO NOT REMOVE YOUR HAT FOR ANY REASON.

After a week or so without shampoo and hot water, hair becomes a mass of angry clumps and wads. These leave the person beneath looking like an escapee from a mental institution. Such an appearance may shake your team's confidence in your judgment.

If you can't shampoo, pull a cap down over your ears and leave it there, night and day, for the entire expedition.

RULE NO. 6: DO NOT ASK
IF ANYBODY'S SEEN YOUR STUFF.

Experienced adventurers have systems for organizing their gear. They very rarely leave it strewn around camp or lying back on the trail. One of the most damning things you can do is ask your teammates if they've seen the tent poles you thought you packed twenty miles ago. Even in the event you get home alive, you will not be invited on the next trip.

Should you ever leave tent poles twenty miles away, do not ask if anybody's seen them. Simply announce—with a good-natured chuckle—that you are about to set off in the dark on a forty-mile hike to retrieve them.

RULE NO. 7: NEVER ASK "WHERE
ARE WE?" OR "HOW MUCH LONGER?"

If you want to know your location, look at a map. Try to figure it out yourself. If you're still confused, feel free to discuss the identities of landmarks around you and how they correspond to the cartography.

Now, if you (a) suspect a mistake has been made *and* (b) have experience reading topographical maps *and* (c) are certain that your leader is a novice or on drugs, speak up. Otherwise, follow the group like a sheep.

RULE NO. 8: CARRY MORE THAN YOUR FAIR SHARE.

When the trip is over, would you rather be remembered fondly as a rock or scornfully as a wussy? Keep in mind that a few extra pounds won't make your pack more painful than it already is.

In any given group of flatlanders, somebody is bound to bicker about weight. When an argument begins, take the extra weight yourself. Shake your head and gaze with pity on the slothful one. This is the mature response to childish behavior. On the trail that day, load the greenhorn's pack with twenty pounds of gravel.

RULE NO. 9: DO NOT GET SUNBURNED.

Sunburn is not only painful and unattractive; it's also an obvious sign of inexperience. Most bozos wait too long before applying sunscreen.

Once you're burned on an expedition, you may not have a chance to get out of the sun. The burn will get burned, skin will peel away, blisters will sprout on the already swollen lips . . . you get the idea.

Wear zinc oxide. You can see exactly where and how thickly it's applied, and it gives you just about 100 percent protection. It does get on your sunglasses, all over your clothes, and in your mouth. But that's OK. Unlike sunshine, zinc oxide is nontoxic.

RULE NO. 10: DO NOT GET KILLED.

Suppose you make the summit of K2 solo, chain-smoking Gitanes and carrying the complete works of Hemingway in hardcover. Macho, huh?

Suppose that you then take a vertical detour into the jaws of a crevasse and never make it back to base camp. Would you still qualify as a hero? And what if you do? No one is going to run any fingers through your new chest hair.

The worst thing to have on your outdoor résumé is a list of the possible locations of your remains. Besides, your demise might distract your team members from enjoying the rest of their vacation.

All expedition behavior flows from one principle: think of your team first. You are merely a cog in that machine. If you're unable to be a good cog, your team will never have more than one member[11]—and you will never achieve suavity.

Java, Man

Some people need coffee to feel human in the morning. These friends of Juan Valdez need not suffer in the woods.

Advertising claims notwithstanding, no brand of instant coffee is even remotely elegant or sophisticated. In fact, none is even vaguely reminiscent of the real thing. All powdered drinks, including cocoa

---

[11]A penile member.

and fruit crystals, get old fast, even in the wilderness. Tea, while soothing, does not offer the jolt of full-bore tarlike java.

Two brewing methods produce authentic joe with minimal extra weight or fuss.

Cowboy Coffee. Ingredients: cold water; one scoop of coffee for the pot and one for each cup.

Place the ingredients in a pot or tin can; bring to a boil and then immediately remove it from the heat. (This recipe has hardly changed since the time of the Incas.) Before pouring, bang on the side of the pot—many of the grounds will sink. By pouring carefully you'll be able to keep most of the grounds out of your cup.

Grounds do, however, add a crunchy, macho texture to coffee. Stuck in your teeth, they will enhance your devil-may-care appearance.

Espresso. Espresso,[12] although less gnarly than cowboy coffee, confers more style on a wilderness breakfast. Single- and double-serving aluminum espresso makers can be found at better kitchen supply stores. Their water and coffee reservoirs screw together to hold a perforated metal cup, which holds the grounds for percolation.

Unused grounds can be stored in plastic bags in the coffee maker when it is not in use. Used grounds must be buried or carried.

An espresso maker adds about a pound to your luggage, but the thick, rich coffee it produces puts a sparkle in your eye and makes you a more attractive

---

[12]An Italian word meaning "Is how I express myself."

person. Not only are you more alert, but you clearly know how to lead a life of luxury despite primitive circumstances. More people will want to hang around near your tent. More of them will want to touch you.

LOVE WITHOUT SHOWERING

The great outdoors whets appetites of all kinds. People become tanned, strong, and relaxed. As they master fear and the elements, they become easier to admire. They share vistas and precious moments of natural wonder. Nobody has to blow fifty bucks on dinner.

Hiking behind a tanned, athletic, outdoorsy person for hours at a time, one's mind easily wanders from that person's well-rounded calves to the lightly skinned knees to the firm thighs and so on.

Love in the wild is harsh, however. After several days of strenuous exercise without bathing or grooming, one begins to look and smell like a Stone Age hominid.

Most of the outdoors is hard and lumpy, very different from the mattress and box spring most people take for granted at home. Nights can be cold. Sleeping bags and even tents are too cramped for vigorous romance.

Of course the walls of even the cheapest hotel room are thicker than a tent's. Privacy can be hard to achieve.

But all of these obstacles to love can be overcome with the proper attitude and technique.

The Back Rub Classic

Hiking or climbing inevitably leads to muscle soreness—and a good excuse for massage. The back rub is ideal because the recipient, lying face down, cannot see the provider's matted hair or various protuberances.

Warm your hands by rubbing them, *not by placing them in your crotch area or armpits*, which will be toxic after several days on the trail. Straddle your prone victim and gently but firmly knead the neck and base of his or her skull. As the subject's tension begins to fade, the subject's shirt will come off more easily.

Always stroking in the direction of the heart, concentrate on the muscles of the shoulders and along the spine. Do not remove either hand from the skin until the massage is over.

Unless you are highly trained, avoid the lats—any tickling will dispel the all-important element of trust. Do not mention any curvature of the spine or large, hairy moles. Dispense plausible compliments instead, such as remarks on the firmness of the muscles, the breadth of the shoulders, the impressive acne scars, etc.

After you have completed your work on the back, shoulder, and neck areas, move to the scalp. Scratch it lightly but firmly with your fingernails and pull the hair gently by running your fingers through it. This should cause your victim to tingle all over and lose his or her better judgment. Wipe the hair grease off your hands.

The total massage can now begin.

The Hypothermia Gambit[13]

Lowering your core temperature produces a dreamy, sleepy state that is not at all unpleasant. As you go beyond chilled and your shivering stops, you will become lethargic, disoriented, and perhaps unhappy about something somebody said to you when you were a child. Then you will go into shock.

Quick action by your partners will now be required to save your life.

The most reliable remedy is a big wiggle[14] with the person in your group you find most attractive. Foreplay is out of the question—this is an emergency.

The Hypothermia Gambit has two considerable risks: your partners' choice of "nurse" may not be your own; and any delay in their recognition of your hypothermia could cause you to lapse into a coma and die.

Privacy

Once they have formed, couples in the wild sometimes have trouble finding enough privacy and comfort to consummate their passion. Blood-sucking insects, prying eyes and ears, sharp rocks, and bad weather can conspire to distract us from love.

The long hike to a remote redoubt is often the best way to find privacy. A mountain meadow burst-

---

[13]Suitable only for people actually *prepared to die* for a piece of ass.
[14]Horizontal bop.

ing with wildflowers can provide a romantic atmo-
sphere powerful enough to make people ignore each
other's stubble and scent.

Watch for especially fertile ground, places that
seem to explode with green. The place may feel dry
when you first lie down but will release water like a
sponge as you bounce around on it.

If you can't get away, try turning simple, every-
day events into romantic interludes:

- A mutual tick check can be a tender moment.

- Offer to hack the clumps from your beloved's
  hair and, out of kindness, sharpen your
  pocketknife especially well before you begin.

- At a safe distance, pretend to revel in your
  partner's rich aroma.

SPOTTING THE COMMON BUBBLEHEAD

In the wilderness every bozo becomes a hazard. Our
safety, comfort, and peace of mind are threatened
by those not attuned to their surroundings.

To avoid fools we must recognize them. Most fall
into general categories and can be identified by
their appearance and behavior.

Boy Scouts

Scouting is preparation for life in the military. Boy
Scouts learn to wear uniforms, follow orders, and

take over territory and neutralize it. Their staging areas can be identified by trenches dug around tent sites, as per Scouting handbooks written in 1949. Scout paths are the ones blazed with hatchet marks. Scouts actually *cut down* trees and build raging bonfires.

Because they travel at battalion strength, Scouts cannot be liquidated en masse without an air strike. The environmentally friendly solution is to scatter them with realistic bear and wolverine sounds outside their tents in the middle of the night. Separated from the herd, individual Scouts can easily drown or "fall" off cliffs. Three or four fatalities are usually enough to cause a Scouting force to retreat from its assault on the wilderness.

Hoods in the Woods

Frustrated parents sometimes force a troubled child into a "wilderness experience." They imagine that fresh air and scenery will distract their kid from sex, drugs, and grand theft auto and will keep the little felon out of trouble for a few weeks.

Unfortunately, the woods are almost entirely free of police officers—the only people qualified to handcuff and beat the crap out of troubled teenagers. We must simply try to recognize and avoid these kids.

A hood-in-the-woods can be identified by a scowl, surly demeanor, excessively pale skin, and bad haircut. Self-inflicted tattoos and skull-oriented jewelry also may signal sociopathic tenden-

THE COOL OF THE WILD

cies. Be sure to keep several miles between you and all potential perpetrators.

The Loner

The typical solo camper (almost invariably male) prides himself on "traveling light." In arctic conditions, for example, he carries chocolate bars instead of food and a tarp instead of a tent. When he gets hungry and cold, he will try to eat your dinner and sleep in your tent with you. When he gets injured, you must decide whether to carry him to the road, let him die, or kill him.

This can be a difficult decision. The soloist is comfortable putting your vacation in jeopardy—it's no wonder he can't find a partner. Offer him directions back to the roadhead and nothing else.

Party Swine

Party pigs view the wilderness as a fresh place to throw up. They are easy to spot—no one else hikes with coolers or stereo equipment. They don't consider wilderness sacred—to them it's nothing more than a big hotel room.

Assaulting a pride of party pigs is ill advised because many of them carry firearms, those natural companions of alcohol. We can avoid swine by traveling into remote areas—anywhere more than three miles from a roadhead should do it. Beer is too heavy to lug very far.

Second Amendment Types

Many hunters seriously believe nature exists for the benefit of man.[15] Where we see a pheasant in flight, they see meat trying to escape. They think their fellow predators, like mountain lions and timber wolves, are vermin to be poisoned and shot. Any vertebrate not wearing orange might as well be wearing a target.

We can avoid hunters by staying indoors, with the shades drawn, during hunting season. Flak jackets and orange clothing are advised for sorties out to the car.

Horse packers can be avoided by staying off trails and sticking to high, rugged terrain. If they give you any trouble, feel free to preserve the centuries-old American tradition of liberating our enslaved brother and sister horses.

Bruces

To the untrained eye, the typical Bruce looks homeless. After all, many Bruces sleep outdoors or in cars year-round. Their smell is often vivid. Constant tanning and infrequent bathing leave them with broad patches of ground-in facial dirt.

Unlike the urban homeless, however, Bruces invariably own a few pieces of fine gear, such as Gore-Tex coveralls, Galibier glacier goggles, fifteen pounds of Friends, and at least one pair of fairly new mountaineering skis.

---

[15]Many think women exist for the same reason.

Bruces have irregular jobs, closed checking accounts, disconnected phone numbers, and no interest in fine dining, hairstyles, or world events. True Bruces have only one true love: the outdoors. While other people buy things, watch TV, and worry about rent, Bruces talk to birds, listen to snow fall, and gradually lose their minds.

On rare occasions you may find them at the ragged edges of civilization, devouring leftovers from tables in fast-food restaurants or sleeping in battered station wagons in remote parking lots.

Like anyone totally devoted to one thing, Bruces tend to be poor conversationalists, but we can still admire their dedication and focus. We can hire them in the off-season to do work outdoors, thus providing them with the few dollars they will need to replace their worn Gore-Tex coveralls and return to their happy exile.

Experts

Unlike bubbleheads, expert campers are hard to spot. They blend in with their surroundings. The only colors they wear are found in the landscape. They would no sooner raise their voices in the wild than they would in a church.

They camp well out of sight of the trail. After they break camp, there is no sign they've been there—no charred rocks, no broken tree limbs, no worn paths. Experts carry out their own garbage and that left by others.

Their packs look neat and are free of dangling objects like shoes and pans. Experts may carry ropes or skis, but they find guns and big knives useless. They may carry a small supply of decent whiskey, but no beer or wine.

Experts keep the oldest American traditions alive by using the wilderness without using it up.

SMELL OF THE WILD

As any expert can tell you, shitting in the woods can be a great pleasure; finding human shit in the woods is always a deep unhappiness.[16] Mindful of the turd's aesthetic paradox, experts use sophisticated methods to maximize pleasure and minimize suffering.

Many four-legged animals, bears in particular, find human fecal matter irresistible. After locating it by smell they will make heroic efforts to dig it up. Such is their joy upon unearthing this treasure that they will spread it over the area, fouling what might have been a decent campsite.

Drinking or even swimming in water contaminated with feces can spoil a vacation within hours and make a person violently ill for weeks.

Turd burial, therefore, is a serious matter. It must be done right. Move a heavy rock to one side and dig a "cat hole" two or three feet deep and more than a hundred feet from water. Dig deeper if people will use it more than five or six times. Save the soil; you will use it to refill the hole. A small tree or stump next to the latrine, acting as a sort of dance-studio bar, can make squatting easier.

---

[16]Used toilet paper can only magnify the horror of such a discovery.

People who insist on using toilet paper must either carry it out or burn it because it is litter. Before leaving the area, return the dirt to the hole and put the rock back to discourage animal excavation projects.

Tearing up a bush to wipe with its leaves is crass. Many experts rely on smooth stones, especially cool, clean stones found in creeks. Some people prefer round stones roughly the size of racquetballs; others scrape with flat stones slightly smaller than playing cards. Certain sticks also work well, especially the spoon-shaped variety.

Soiling the Treeless Regions

Alpine and polar regions may offer no shelter for the modest, but even the most bashful person must eventually answer the call. Few fellow campers will *want* to watch, of course; announcing your intention is usually enough to make them look the other way.

When the wind blows like the unleashed dogs of hell, novices may hesitate to swing their bare anatomy into the air. Nature intended us to do so, however, and provided the right equipment.

The human butt's sheath of fat acts not only as a seat cushion but also as a permanent butt parka. You can squat down and point your buns into a gale-force wind at −20° F, and the feeling is rather refreshing.

But real winter refreshment comes in the form of snowballs. They are so much better than toilet paper that you may decide to install a freezer in your bathroom when you get home.

When in an arctic region, remember that turds will be preserved where you leave them. Left on a glacier or some other essentially permanent snowfield, they may be preserved for thousands of years. Your shit may interest archaeologists someday, but in the meantime, do future campers a favor and deposit it in a hole at least two feet deep. Don't forget that people will be melting that snow for drinking water for many years after you are gone.

Aiming to Please

Some animals crave salt so badly that you may see them eating dirt. These unfortunate creatures will be so thrilled to find your urine on a bush that they will eat it. One poorly aimed squirt of pee may result in an innocent bush's untimely death. Experts pee on rocks or sandy places well away from water.

HARASSING AND KILLING DEFENSELESS CREATURES

Not everyone feels sorry for animals, even those who eat pee-covered bushes. Humans go so far as to kill animals, even wild animals, for three basic reasons: we're hungry, bored, or irritated.

Breakfast of Animals

Once in a great while you may find yourself with a loaded weapon but no garden, no money, no credit, and no food stamps. In this prehistoric situation you may get hungry enough to kill another animal and eat its corpse.

For culinary reasons, you don't want to direct so much firepower at another creature that it is completely shredded. Nor do you wish to simply wound an animal—it will suffer, bleed all over the place, and possibly escape. Therefore you must match your weapon and ammunition to the animal.

Rocks, bows and arrows, and handguns do not have the power or accuracy at long range to make a meal reasonably likely.

Assault weapons such as the AR-15, M-16, and AK-47 are equally useless. Their high-velocity bullets are designed not to put steaks in the freezer but to liquefy human flesh and bone upon impact.

The best weapons for hunting food, therefore, range from a shotgun to a standard hunting rifle such as the .30-caliber carbine. Plastic-coated and other "cop killer" bullets will be necessary only when ducks and deer start wearing little flak jackets.

Animals as "Game"

An ancient urge throbs in the guts of man—to chase a furry thing through the woods, to slay that thing, and to bind its lifeless body to the hood of a late-model car.

Unfortunately, we have killed nearly all the fierce furry things and left only docile vegetarians like deer, birds, and squirrels. They fall easily under a hail of bullets, rarely trying to bite us or seriously challenge our manhood. For real excitement we must either make killing our native fauna more difficult or find more dangerous animals to kill.

Bow hunting is a challenge because the hunter has to get within six or seven feet of an animal to have much hope of killing it. Ideally the razor-sharp edges of the arrowhead slice open one of the creature's major arteries and the animal bleeds to death internally. More commonly, the prey is startled into motion by the hunter drawing his bow, causing him to miss his mark and shoot the animal in the butt. It then runs off and, after a week or so, dies of an infection.

Killing deer with bows and arrows or pistols obviously requires great skill, as does golf, plus a manly disregard for the suffering of fellow creatures. But deer hunting, like golf, is a game, not a sport, because the hunter faces no danger from the quarry.

For hunting to be a sport, the prey must have a fair chance of turning the tables and killing the hunter. The following matchups qualify as sporting:

ANIMAL	FIELD OF HONOR	MAXIMUM FIREPOWER
Cape buffalo	African swamp	snub-nosed .38
wild boar	thick brush	baseball bat
angry wolverine	outhouse	Sears catalog
grizzly or polar bear	open tundra or pack ice	sharp stick

Vermin

Some animals interfere with our comfort and some with our business ventures. We kill them not for food or sport but out of practicality and malice.

The female mosquito[17] holds the title of high priestess of pests, carrying misery to every wet, warm corner of the land.

While the individual mosquito is fragile and foolhardy, the genus is as durable as granite. With that in mind we should preserve our dignity and resist flailing at mosquitoes no matter how thickly they fill the air. Rugged people should not sit around slapping their own faces. The stronger brands of repellent discourage most mosquitoes; six-legged desperadoes can be stopped with netting.

Mosquitoes prefer tourists to nasty, dirty outdoor people. Freshly scrubbed skin and expensive perfume make the insects drool with anticipation. Grease, sweat, ground-in filth, and frequent farting, on the other hand, cause mosquitoes to lose their appetites. They are naturally dainty creatures.

Unfortunately, blackflies, found in the far north around the world in early summer, are anything but dainty. Rather than dip and flutter, blackflies rocket and crawl like tiny armored soldiers. Instead of sticking and sipping, they slash and sop, leaving a bleeding, easily infected wound. They can ignore any repellent and slip under netting. They don't mind BO, DDT, or other nerve agents. They hardly

---

[17] *Irritatus nonstopus.*

notice flamethrowers. The only effective defense is a plane ticket.

Rabbits, moles, foxes, groundhogs, prairie dogs, crows, hawks, and other animals sometimes spoil the plans of people who count chickens and admire lawns. Killing "vermin" is never sporting.

HOW NOT TO ACT
IN FRONT OF A LARGE WILD ANIMAL

A few dozen times a year animals turn the tables on human beings. They will attack us for three basic reasons: they're hungry, they're scared, or we piss them off. Distinguishing these attitudes is the first step toward avoiding unsightly teeth marks.

People as Food

Crocodiles, big bears, and tigers are among the few animals who regularly look at us and see lunch.

If you see one of these predators, consider yourself lucky and *stay in your vehicle. Do not attempt to feed, pet, or hug any man-eating animal.* Upon seeing a tiger, tourists think it "looks like Kitty." A tiger thinks tourists "look like gerbils."

If you're on foot when you encounter a tiger or polar bear, one of you is basically dead. If you aren't carrying a loaded large-bore firearm, that would basically be you.

If you're in the water and meet one or more big crocodiles, do not feel ashamed to soil yourself. A small croc, one less than twelve feet long, will grasp

THE COOL OF THE WILD

you in its jaws and smile while it holds you under until you drown. Then it will stuff you under a log for a few days until you soften up.

Crocodile teeth can only grasp; they can't carve, as can those of cats and bears. Pairs of smaller crocs solve this problem by grasping you at opposite ends and rolling, twisting off bite-size pieces. Large crocs, such as those twenty feet long, are powerful enough to rip your extremities off without letting you rot first. Some swallow people whole.

Some experts say crocodiles are startled or confused by "tall" prey. If you can get to shallow water and rise up above the animal, it might pause long enough for you to make a brief confession, such as "I'm sorry," before it dismembers you.

People as Pests

Billions of animals are pissed off by people, and you can't blame them. Most of us are smarter than animals, have better jobs, and take longer vacations. They can sense these things.

All carnivores infected with rabies, and a few vegetarians, such as hippos and elephants, are fearless animals regularly irritated by humans. People in special danger include

- anyone wearing cologne, a Rolex, or a Ralph Lauren safari outfit;

- anyone who has handled a "capture net" for Jacques Cousteau or Marlin Perkins;

- anyone who is timid or overconfident.

Respecting animals is difficult. Take elephants, for example: they have thick ankles. Wolverines can't seem to relax—they're always *hurtling*. Warthogs have extremely bad breath. Nevertheless, we must accept that each species represents a strand woven into the Vast Tapestry of Life.

As a mental exercise, compare a squirrel, any squirrel, to Jerry Falwell. Which would you rather have living in your attic?

Let's face it: the worst qualities of human beings are far more noxious than those of other creatures. This knowledge leads to the humility that will help protect you from large, fearless animals. You won't feel compelled to stare them down, for example, which aggravates them. Bowing and otherwise looking small and insignificant will help your chances of survival at close quarters. Whenever possible, keep your distance.

People as Peril

Billions of animals are terrified of people, and you can't blame them. Most of us demand the deaths of animals for fashion reasons alone. Naturally, every self-respecting animal wants to bite off key parts of your anatomy, inject you with poison, squish your head like a grape, break you in half, and electrocute you.

There are far too many self-respecting animals to list here; they range from scorpions, spiders, and snakes to raccoons, stray dogs, and moose.

If you encounter a frightened and dangerous animal, reassure it that you mean no harm and that you are not like other people it may have met. Do not make any sudden movements. Back away slowly and use gentle, calming phrases like "How pretty you are!" and "Nice black mamba!" Leave the area.

BUILD YOUR OWN DANGER DOG

Some animals are our friends. The right danger dog, a rare and precious animal, can save your neck in the woods. It will smell a grizzly before you do. It will keep you warm in a bivouac. It will catch fish for breakfast. It will test steep slopes for avalanche danger without insisting on a belay.[18]

The wrong animal, the devil dog, will follow only those commands issued while it is being actively choked. Unleashed in the wilderness, its eyes will become crossed and it will bark ceaselessly, chase every living creature it encounters, including porcupines and skunks, abandon you to run with the wolves, not find any, get bitten by raccoons, contract rabies, and hunt you down and kill you.

Some people don't know their animals are devil dogs. For this reason many wise bureaucrats forbid dogs in wilderness areas, where they frighten and kill woodland creatures and sometimes become feral nuisances.[19] Before you take a dog into the woods, think carefully about how often it obeys you and whether it is the right dog for the job.

---

[18]May require strong encouragement. A danger dog is not a stupid dog.
[19]The dogs, not the bureaucrats.

Some people insist the standard poodle is loyal, intelligent, and fierce. They should stay out of the woods.

Others like the basset hound's easygoing nature and tracking ability. Nonlawn terrain can be a problem, however: a side of bacon can outjump the average basset.

Many Dobermans and pit bulls are eager to drink Bambi blood. Rottweilers and Great Danes sink in fresh snow and get chilly. Mastiffs, wolfhounds, and St. Bernards are so big you'd need porters to carry their kibble.

The best all-purpose danger dog is something of a mutt. To create the ideal animal, combine the following ingredients:

- one-quarter shepherd for loyalty and obedience

- one-quarter wolf for a tall, lean physique, heavy coat, and snowshoelike paws

- one-quarter mastiff or rottweiler for windpipe-crushing death grip

- one-quarter border collie for understanding of the English language, including all the days of the week, the difference between *who* and *whom*, and proper use of the subjunctive

Extreme Skiing

ARCHETYPE PROFILE: SKIING ACE

Appearance: Nut-brown face and
hands, tofu-white neck and arms.

Home: Carbondale, Colorado.

House: Tar paper 'n' two-by-four.

Occupation: Aspen emergency medical
technician.

Favorite Clothing: North Face
jumpsuit, goofy Peruvian alpaca hat.

Thighs: Concrete.

Ideal Date: Bottle of schnapps, hot tub,
nude snowball fight with head of
ski school.

Goal: Staying wild 'n' free.

Worst Fear: Moving back to
Des Moines.

CORRECT CLOTHING VS. EAST GEEKVILLE

To ski like a disembodied spirit a person's got to be comfortable. To be comfortable a person's got to be warm and dry. In skiwear, as in Zen, function and form are one. Cotton clothing, for example, is impractical for skiing. In terms of function—to absorb water and keep a body cool—it is worse than useless in winter. Moronic function means moronic form. Jeans and sweatshirts make skiers look like morons or, in extreme cases,[20] like hicks.[21]

Rules are made to be broken, of course. Skiers might wear cotton shorts on a warm day in the spring without looking like dorks if they ski gracefully and very fast.

As in many human endeavors, the master is permitted to make and break the rules. The best skiers on the mountain can get away with wearing tuxedos, gorilla outfits, or one-piece Day-Glo spandex suits. The rest of us should wear things that serve some purpose other than getting us noticed.

Adaptability and Flexibility

Unless you happen to be skiing someplace where the weather never changes, you'll want to wear clothes in layers that can be peeled away in warmer conditions.

---

[20]Such as those involving leather jackets.
[21]Texans.

The best skiwear has built-in flexibility. A fine parka shell, for example, will be roomy enough to breathe but have drawstrings and Velcro to make it snug in the waist, neck, and wrists when necessary. It will also have a hood with a drawstring and arm vents that can be unzipped to air out the pits during exercise. The shell alone may cost you more than $400.

To be cold is to have failed as an outdoorsperson. A skilled adventurer is always comfortable in a ski resort setting.

Color

If we go around shouting, *"Hey, look at me! Am I not the absolute intensest?"* we had better be good at what we're doing. If we are indeed TSM,[22] a few people might give us half an ounce of grudging respect, but we will make no friends. People who don't even know us will try to divorce us and sue our asses for alimony and child support.

This phenomenon, known as the Cassius Clay Syndrome, teaches us one lesson: if we are not the greatest skier on the mountain, we do not wear loud ski clothing.

HOW TO SKI THE TREES AT HIGH SPEED

Once we are properly dressed, we head for the trees. Much of the snow blown from ski slopes settles in

---

[22]The Supreme Master.

nearby woods. Protected from the corrupting rays of the sun and the flailing of novices, powder can retain its virginity for more than a week.

Unlocking this secret store of powder can extract a high price. Trees are stern ski instructors in a course called Stark Reality. They are not as flexible as they look. Paraplegia and death are real possibilities.

But mastering fall-line tree skiing is one of the great pleasures of the outdoors. Terror is transformed from a paralyzing inertia into power and clarity. Showing off is impossible—the skier's grace is obscured by the forest, witnessed only by the Great Spirit. The skier's sex organs not only shrivel but may actually retreat deep into body cavities in an effort to protect themselves.

Many pine trees bristle with squaw wood—dead, pointy lower boughs—which can shred the finest skiwear and penetrate the thickest skull. These trees are also warm enough to melt the snow around them and create holes to swallow unwary skiers.

Trees and deep snow also swallow the cries of the wounded. If you can't get out on your own, no one may find your body until spring.

Upon entering the forest, many expert skiers are reminded of their first days on snow. The body tends to stiffen; ski tips point together in a humiliating snowplow; turning becomes difficult if not impossible. It's like starting over, and the techniques are the same: (1) start on a relatively shallow slope; (2) bend your knees; (3) relax your muscles, especially those in your face.

Start in a grove of well-spaced older aspen trees if possible. Aspen have no squaw wood and have shallower holes around their bases.

As an expert you can turn whenever you must. To ski the trees you have to believe that and do it without hesitation. Grace defines the master.

As you enter the Realm of Mastery, you will ski the virgin powder of steep, uncut forest slopes at high speed, unable to see more than two turns—less than two seconds—ahead of you, and yet somehow you will burst from the woods without a scratch. You will have tasted the immortality of the eternal present and will probably be thirsty for a beer.

The World of the Compound Fracture

Because mastery can sometimes elude even the best of us, wise tree skiers invest in major medical coverage with no upper limit. Some spend the better part of their lives wheeling around managed-care facilities, babbling about the Norse god of weather and drooling on themselves.

Besides spinal and head injuries, a common result of tree skiing is the compound fracture. When the inside of a bone is exposed to air, it looks really neat, but it can become infected and cause the loss of the limb. Do not try to push the bone back inside yourself, even if you can do it without hurling.

The femoral artery runs along the femur, the thighbone. Breaking the femur is especially perilous because the jagged bone can tear the artery and cause massive internal bleeding. The thigh muscles, the largest in the body, contract when the femur breaks, creating a powerful shearing effect and pain that can be relieved only by major surgery, weeks of traction, and morphine.

People who fail to ski trees properly sometimes get their femurs broken. The ski patrol knows how to put a leg in traction. The ski patrol knows how to tie a tourniquet. The ski patrol carries full liability insurance. In case of an immobilizing injury, call the ski patrol. Do not "try" any medical procedure you haven't studied and practiced, even if the victim is screaming at you to do something.

Name-Dropper's Note

Crested Butte, Colorado, has some of the best lift-served tree skiing anywhere. With more than twenty ungroomed double-black-diamond runs, the area is a Mecca for hard-to-scare experts from around the country.

The downtown area, a national historic district, has been spared the worst of the condomania that has infected other major Rocky Mountain ski resorts.

Crested Butte is about four hours by car from Denver, the nearest city, so the resort never gets very crowded. There are so few skiers with the *cojones* to ski the double-black-diamond runs that there's never a line for the lift that serves them.

THE SEARCH FOR POWDER

There may be many ways to reach a blessed state on skis, but one element is always required: good snow, preferably thigh-deep powder with the weight and flavor of winter sunshine.

To a flatlander, powder like that may seem as rare as yeti. No one can say when it will appear, and it seems to disappear almost immediately. Mountain weather is notoriously unpredictable, even over a matter of hours, and most of us plan our ski trips weeks, if not months, in advance. Strategies do exist to increase the chances of getting good snow, however. The first step, of course, is finding it.

Snow Detection

It's difficult even to know when Holy Grail–type snow has fallen somewhere because official reports don't have the vocabulary to describe it. Eskimos are said to have a thousand words for snow, but ski resorts, looking after their own interests, use only three terms: *powder*, *packed powder*, and *corn*. Their strict policy is never to use words like *slush*, *ice*, *grass*, or *gravel*. Likewise, the official depth report is expressed as a single figure, such as "forty-eight inches," that fails to represent the variety of depths on the mountain.

The best clues to snow quality in official sources are found in the closed-slope report. Slopes are closed most often because bare ground is exposed and runs need snow to heal.

The steepest pitches are typically the last to be skiable and the first to get "skied off." Conditions may still be adequate for intermediates when the only slopes closed are those meant for experts. When intermediate slopes are closed, however, the snow situation truly is dire. Would-be skiers will want to have packed a few good books in their luggage. Rain gear may also be useful.

If all slopes are open, adequate cover is almost guaranteed, but good snow is not. Luckily, reliable sources of snow information can be found at every ski resort: ski bums. Despite reports of their demise, they survive in their traditional positions in the lowest depths of service industries.

Cooks, waiters, bartenders, and front-desk people cannot qualify as ski bums because their jobs require experience and dedication. Few of them ski every day. True ski bums are dedicated only to the mountain. If they have jobs at all, they shovel snow, wash dishes, or clean hotel rooms.

Shovelers and dishwashers are difficult to reach by phone, but housekeepers can be reached in the early morning at the big hotels. Simply call the main number and ask for Housekeeping.

Give your first name to the person who answers and use the Suave-Matic Reference Guide to communicate.

A Suave-Matic fact-finding effort cuts through the vagueness and outright obfuscation of official ski reports. The inside scoop will help you avoid an expensive vacation blunder.

By making regular calls to Housekeeping, you can track conditions and be ready when snow flies.

SUAVE-MATIC QUICK
REFERENCE GUIDE: SKI SPEAK

STATEMENT	MEANING
So, like, dude. Is it true what I heard? Rocks up top?	Hello, my friend. Has much of the snow blown off the mountain?
They're, like, not too rasty, but I had to make four welds last week. That was like half my paycheck.	Not entirely, but I have severely damaged my skis, which are more important to me than eating or paying rent.
Harsh. I heard they were, like, grazing sheep on Elevator Shaft.	My deep sympathies, comrade. Does grass truly grow on the steep slopes?
Yeah, but two weeks ago was stupid sweet. Ill. Wait. Maybe that was, like, three weeks ago. Whatever.	Yes, but snow is a fine and temporal thing. We have tasted of its essence this season.
They talking about a dump anytime soon, man?	Do you expect a return of the ephemeral crystals?

Continued

STATEMENT	MEANING
Hey, like we *talk* about it, but Ullr's on vacay, I guess.	If the good Lord will get off His butt.
Watch it, mon. He might hear you.	Do not blaspheme the Deity if you wish His blessing, friend.

Flexible Reservations

When your sources tell you that big snow has arrived, it's time to head for the mountains. People with regular jobs may find the boss reluctant to see them go on vacation with only an hour's notice. Calling in sick is not usually an option; the inevitable skiing tan—tomato red from the neck up—is a dead giveaway. The best approach to a job/snow conflict is to quit the job.

Buying a plane ticket in advance does lower vacation costs, but skiing is so expensive today that plane tickets are cheaper than ever in relation to the rest of the trip. The basic arithmetic in the chart on the opposite page shows what we mean:

Multiply that for a five-day ski vacation, and the cost is $1,591.25, plus about $350 round-trip airfare from anywhere to the Rockies, the place most likely to feature supreme powder. Skis, boots, poles, hats, goggles, parkas, ski pants, ski sweaters, ski socks, ski underwear, ski sunscreen, extra-alcoholic ski beverages, and orthopedic ski surgery are extra.

Paying that kind of money for ice or gravel can lead only to unhappiness.

Your skiing technique does not have a chance to improve on bad snow because you must be on alert for protruding granite or Zamboni-slick patches of ice. You become discouraged, quit early each day, and retire to the lodge, where you consume entire wheels of special ski resort cheeses, slapping four to six pounds of flab onto your body *every hour.*

Compare that Joblike suffering to the Spontaneous Ski Vacation. Of all the costs, only the airfare rises, to about $750. The difference of $400 is only slightly more expensive than a single day of skiing, and you actually *save* money on ski repair bills and base lodge breakfasts.

The snow is so good that you leap out of bed at

Breakfast at base lodge	$19.50
Lift ticket	45.00
Lunch on mountain	28.95
Après-ski cocktails	24.95
Ski repair bill (when snow is poor)	49.95
Quitting-job celebration dinner	79.95
Hotel room (per person)	69.95
Total cost of one day of skiing	$318.25

dawn and grab granola bars on your way out of your room, skipping breakfast in your race for the lifts.

As you glide and punch your way through the exceptional powder, your body becomes leaner and stronger. Your skiing ability improves: you reach previously unimagined levels of grace and understanding. You stop shaving, and your hair becomes matted. Finally, airborne in slow motion, you achieve a timeless moment beyond perfection.

The job you abandoned is no longer relevant in your private universe. The extra $400 you spent on airfare means no more to you than a sparkling wisp of spindrift.

That's a vacation.

Prayer

Should you arrive at a ski area and, despite clever intelligence gathering and a bold career strategy, find a dearth of snow, there is no harm in prayer.

Ullr (pronounced "Earl" with a sort of low growl), the Norse god of weather, is thought to respond favorably to potent offerings from cold climates, such as Scandinavian vodka and the better brands of schnapps. A slug of the chosen potion should be slopped out of one's glass, preferably onto a good carpet, while making humble entreaties to the busy deity.[23]

[23] *Warning:* Ullr is thought to heap misfortune on mortals presumptuous enough to predict mountain weather. Any talk of possible snow must be expressed in terms of hope, not likelihood.

Try this sample snow prayer:

O Most Unstoppable and Omnipotent Storm-
  Meister, Closer of Roads and Airports,
We admired the sunny skies you delivered today,
  thank you extremely, don't get us wrong,
  Mighty Bearded One,
But we hope fervently for a mighty avalanche of
  champagne powder, your Towering Cumulosity,
Beginning before midnight tonight and not letting
  up until about ten tomorrow morning,
If it please you, O Great Muffler of Bugaboos and
  Stratospheric Party Dudicle.

If snow still doesn't fall and conditions remain poor, think about the things you did wrong. Might you have made even an oblique weather prediction? Did you bemoan warm weather or sunshine? Did you wear ski clothing with any colors not found in nature? If so, the fault is your own. Keep the faith, hone your snow strategies, polish your résumé, and maybe you'll have better luck next year.

Name-Dropper's Note

A decent resort operation offers more than fifteen hundred acres of skiing. In British Columbia's Selkirks, Monashees, or Cariboos, a decent heli-ski operation offers more than fifteen hundred *square miles* of skiing, most of it virgin wilderness you don't have to share with anyone except the other rich, tanned, highly skilled skiers in your party.

Doing the Big Steep and Deep

If you ever do get lucky enough to ski chest-deep powder, you're going to have one hell of a hard time plowing through it unless you're on an especially steep slope. It's what every expert skier aspires to: falling through space on an endless serpentine inscription in virgin powder. It's not as easy as it looks, of course. Relax, bend your knees, keep your back straight, and ski like you're riding a slow-motion pogo stick to heaven.

Extreme Wetness

ARCHETYPE PROFILE:
ACE RIVER RUNNER

Appearance: Body in good shape,
clothes fading fast.
Home: Lees Ferry, Arizona.
House: Shared with five other people.
Forearms: Like bunches of twisted
steel cables with a tan.
Latest Nonsport Accomplishment:
Getting into the pants of the
new housemate.
Favorite Clothing: Nude.
Other Skills: Fly fishing; removing
hooks from tender areas.
Worst Fear: Severe drought.

FOOLBOAT

Anyone who's seen the Grand Canyon can begin to appreciate the Power of gravity and water: they can join forces to hammer not just through solid rock but also through large western states. It's enough to make people give up their winter wonderlands and never look back.

Running rapids like those of the Colorado River requires a special combination of reckless lunacy and Zen.

Boat is like the insect-sized flake of balsa wood; river is like the ten thousand fire hoses.

If a good-size state like Arizona can't resist the Power, Grasshopper obviously can't either. Grasshopper must work *with* Power.

Unlike most other games, river running regularly kills people who know all the moves and make them perfectly. A single gallon of water weighs more than eight pounds. A class IV or V river can flow at thousands of gallons per second in every direction. That kind of river can overwhelm even the best paddlers and the buoyancy and integrity of their boats and bodies.

Water's serpentine qualities create dangers for boaters in the form of "holes" (essentially liquid tornadoes), undercuts, and "sweepers," submerged trees, all of which can pin valuable objects underwater.

River runners scout rapids carefully before venturing into them, but savage, boulder-choked rivers can be difficult to read simply by looking at their surfaces. Undercuts and sweepers can be invisible from above.

Chances of survival decrease where rescue is impossible; many of the best sets of rapids pound through deep gorges, such as the Grand Canyon, where daredevil scuba-equipped rescue squads are scarce.

Name-Dropper's Note

The baidarka, the traditional handmade Aleutian kayak, presents a deep mystery to boatbuilders and hydrophysicists. Baidarkas are wider and heavier than modern kayaks and covered with comparatively rough skin or canvas instead of space-age polymers, yet the Aleutian-style kayaks, even when built and paddled by a non-Aleut, are considerably faster. No one knows why.

The Kayak

Kayaks are good for running serious white water because of their high maneuverability upside down. Kayakers prefer not to maneuver upside down, however, because it requires them to hold their breath while their heads get slammed repeatedly on boulders.

In theory, flipped kayaks can be righted with a

maneuver known as an *eskimo roll*. In extreme cases they can be abandoned, but running big rapids without a boat can damage important body parts.

Unfortunately, abandoning a kayak is sometimes impossible. Pinned against rocks or trees underwater, a boat can collapse and fold up or "wrap," trapping the paddler inside.

Kayaking is too dull for some people, so they turn to different craft.

The Inflatable Raft

There are two basic types of rafts: the motor-equipped goofy army surplus kind and the smaller, rowed kind. A goof raft can carry as many as twenty people and is flexible enough to mold itself over standing waves up to ten feet tall. Passengers are free to confront their terror directly, without the distractions of rowing or steering.

A goof raft flips only when the pilot, who is supposed to know the river well, experiences serious lapses in judgment and steering.

The smaller, rowed raft does not mold over big waves; it launches over them. Bucking like a bull, it will throw rowers into the colossal Cuisinart of a raging river. A raft is generally more stable than a kayak but ejects everyone when it flips and is extremely difficult to right in midstream.

In a class IV or V river, a small raft is usually more dangerous than a kayak but slightly less dangerous than driving a propane truck off a cliff.

GREAT BIG WATER 'N' HAZARDS

RIVER	LOCATION	SPECIAL HAZARDS
Colorado	Arizona	Tourists with sun poisoning who need to be evacuated. Immediately. By you.
Colca	Peru	Guerrillas with a uniquely idiotic Maoist philosophy who execute anyone they suspect is North American.
Amazon	Brazil	Electric rays, electric eels, angry Indians, fish up your urethra, etc.
Bío-Bío	Chile	Cops who know only three phrases in English: "Your passport," "You got a reel preety mouth," and "Squeel like a peeg."
Rufiji	Tanzania	Hippos so nasty and enormous they make tiger sharks seem like house pets.

SUAVE-MATIC QUICK
REFERENCE GUIDE: RIVER SPEAK

STATEMENT	MEANING
It's a steep creek.	It falls four hundred feet per mile.
In Section 1, Billy Bob ran the forty-foot drop upside down.	In Section 1, Billy Bob just about had his head removed.
He earned his hairboating license with that maneuver.	Now he gets respect around the campfire.
Section 2 has a couple of deep holes, and staying on line can be difficult.	If you don't follow the correct route, you can get buried underwater.
People have been known to get a couple of lungfuls of water.	Not everyone makes it.
How good *is* your eskimo roll?	Maybe you should stick to lakes for now.

The Canoe

In brutal rapids, canoes exhibit two exhilarating qualities: they turn like aircraft carriers and flip like teacups. Remember *Deliverance:* canoes vs. wild river = bows and arrows vs. shotguns.

Filled with water, canoes weigh a couple of tons and squash swimmers with remarkable ease. They can be carried on portages more easily than rafts, and that comes in handy because there's a lot of water nobody should run in a canoe.

The Rowboat

The first people known to have run the Colorado through the Grand Canyon used two dories, also known as *rowboats*, in 1869. From the standpoint of maximum adventure the craft were nearly perfect: heavy and difficult to maneuver, they offered the buoyancy of deceased dairy cows when upside down.

The leader of the gang, Major John Wesley Powell, had difficulty rowing in a straight line because he had lost an arm in the Civil War. He also lacked swimming skills.

Although these men had seen and even endured unspeakable horrors in the Civil War, including amputations without anesthesia, some of the rapids on the Colorado made them want to pee in their pants.

Two decided to walk home and were never seen again. According to legend, they encountered Native Americans, used pantomime to explain what they

---

Name-Dropper's Note

A rafting trip on the Zambezi River starts at Victoria Falls, on the border between Zambia and Zimbabwe. No one has yet rafted the falls, as they are 350 feet high, but the first day does include ten of the biggest rapids anywhere.

Besides having some of the world's most gut-wrenching white water, the Zambezi contains hippos, which attack and kill more people[24] than do the twenty-foot man-eating crocodiles that also live in the river.

---

had been doing, and were immediately tortured to death to prevent their genes from being passed along to innocent children.

Powell and survivors managed to get home by continuing downriver, largely on foot. If propane trucks had existed in his day, Powell would have driven them over cliffs for his health.

People still row dories down the Colorado today. Some even *pay* to do this.

IT'S A JUNGLE

Some people don't get enough adrenaline from riding a raging river; they have to ride a raging river through a jungle. Jungle environments are so com-

---

[24]Primarily boaters.

petitive that even the plants kill each other. Of the few animals that consider human flesh food, many make their homes and dinners in the jungle, including tigers, jaguars, and crocodiles.

Scores of other jungle species are afraid of everything all the time. They'll bite you just to be on the safe side. Perfectly camouflaged venomous snakes and baseball-size spiders fall into this category.

Leeches drop down on you from the trees to suck your blood. Vampire bats hobble into your shelter, carve you up, and leave you with rabies. Fungi scientists haven't even named bloom on every surface and in every orifice of your person.

ARCHETYPE PROFILE:
ACE JUNGLE EXPLORER

Appearance: Chunky, pale, disheveled.
Home: London and Shropshire, England.
Houses: Vast, old, well kept.
Education: Two years at King's College, Oxford.
Employment: God, no.
Other Skills: Travel writing.
Ideal Date: Hunting, killing, cooking, and eating a giant catfish with two stark naked twelve-year-old Yanomami virgins.
Worst Fear: Fish lodged in urethra.

The candirú, a tiny Amazonian fish that usually lives and lays eggs in the gill cavities of other fish, is perfectly happy to follow a stream of urine, swim up your urethra, and stick out its gills, blocking the passage. Men must choose between the worst possible amputation and death. Women, with nothing to amputate, must wait for their bladders to pop.

And if the animals aren't contrary enough, there are diseases and numerous worm-type parasites that hurt even to think about. Worst of all, the jungle is inhabited by other people. With the severe lack of landmarks, getting lost is inevitable. Without a local guide you're sure to stumble into a place you aren't welcome. The law of the jungle does not provide you with any rights.

Armed miners in the Amazon and Myanmar go crazy from a combination of cheap whiskey, starchy diets, and mercury poisoning. They become paranoid, especially if they've found any gold or jewels, and they can't stand vacationers.

Many Amazon Indians can't stand visitors either, and you can't blame them, given what's been happening for the past five hundred years. Even if they like you they might want you to play one of their party games like Let's Club Each Other in the Head Until Somebody's Brains Squirt Out.

Though Amazon Indians are not fond of jaguars, venomous snakes, or smallpox, two things really scare them: (1) electric rays that shock *and* stab you with six-inch venomous barbs two hundred miles from the nearest hospital and (2) electric eels closely resembling forty-pound intestinal parasites that knock you unconscious, causing you to drown and be eaten by piranha.

INVASION OF THE MICRO-ALIENS

Intestinal parasites can render even the toughest explorer 100 percent suaveless. The first signs of most infections include fever, abdominal pain, and death farts.

The more earnest miniature critters do not respond to Third World medicine—no matter how bitter the retreat, the parasites' human host or hostess must admit defeat and go home immediately. Without proper medical care, some microbes can cause chronic illness, permanent injury, or extinction.

La Tourista

Other names: The trots, the shits, Hershey squirts, old butt-scorcher, Montezuma's diet plan.

Locale: Any country where they use the same word for "raw sewage" and "fertilizer."

Cause: Unfamiliar local bacteria.

Prevention: Avoid uncooked foods that have been touched, breathed on, or looked at by locals. Do not let locals put their hands in your mouth. Drink only bottled water you open yourself or boiled water you boil yourself for at least five minutes—longer at high altitude.

Water may be made potable by pumping it

through a sophisticated filter, but some microbes and most poisons in solution will pass through filters.

Symptoms: Diarrhea, abdominal cramps, fever.

Prognosis: One to four days of suffering.

Cure/Treatment: Passage of time.

Warning: Diarrhea is the body's way of spewing out noxious substances. Lomotil, Immodium, and other antidiarrheal medicines, by slowing the spewing process, may make the illness last longer.

Cholera

Other names: *Vibrio cholerae, O. calcutta.*

Locale: Wherever you find corpse-flavored drinking water.

Cause: Bacterial infection of small intestine from unsanitary water or food, or shellfish that survived severe pollution just long enough to become the daily special.

Prevention: Vaccine imparts partial immunity for six months.

Symptoms: Huge blasts of watery diarrhea and rapid dehydration that may lead to death within hours.

Prognosis: Not good. Symptoms begin within one to five days of infection. Fluids drain out of blood and into intestinal tract.

Cure/Treatment: Aggressive rehydration therapy. Antibiotics will shorten the infectious period.

Dengue Fever

Other names: Breakbone fever, jesus-you-look-like-hell.

Locale: Southeast Asia, Pacific, Central and South America, Africa, Mexico, Puerto Rico, U.S. Virgin Islands, Gulf Coast.

Cause: Bite of female *Aedes aegypti* mosquito.

Prevention: If you see a female *Aedes aegypti* mosquito, spank it to death.

Symptoms: Five to eight days of fever, rash, and severe joint and muscle pain.

Prognosis: You'll live. Probably.

Cure/Treatment: No cure available. Aspirin for pain.

Dysentery

Other names: Shigellosis (bacillary dysentery); amebic dysentery; old-serrated-knife-in-the-guts, ticket home.

Locale: Anyplace people can't afford toilet paper.

Cause: Shigella bacteria (bacillary) or *Entamoeba histolytica* (amebic parasite).

Prevention: Same as *la tourista*.

Symptoms: Stephen King–type diarrhea featuring blood, mucus, and pus.

Prognosis: Amebic dysentery is more serious because it can become chronic.

Cure/Treatment: Trip home and plenty of metronidazole.

Warning: The main danger of dysentery is dehydration. Avoid alcohol and diuretics such as coffee and other caffeinated drinks. Most hospitals, even those in remote areas, will have rehydration drink mixes available, essentially sugars and salts. Never allow locals to prepare these mixes because they may use the same water that made you sick in the first place.

Giardiasis

Other names: Little one-celled buddies.

Locale: Fresh water.

Cause: *Giardia lamblia,* protozoan parasites from hell.[25] They infect the small intestine.

Prevention: Serious boiling or filtering of all water that will come near your mouth.

Symptoms: Greasy, unusually foul-smelling Linda Blair–type feces that float. Also nausea, pain, and cramps.

Prognosis: Victims will be sick for weeks; they must go home.

---

[25]Magnified ten thousand times, they look remarkably like Ed Meese.

Cure/Treatment: Metronidazole or quinacrine will relieve symptoms.

Warning: Two-thirds of victims will have no symptoms but will be able to spread giardiasis in their feces. As a general rule it's best not to take anyone's feces in your mouth, even if the person appears to be healthy.

Hepatitis A

Other names: An inflammation[26] of the liver.[27]

Locale: Anywhere visited by human beings.

Cause: Viral infection from food, water, or interpersonal contact; overdose of certain drugs, including acetaminophen and alcohol.

Prevention: Gamma globulin shots; avoiding restaurants where the employees don't wash their hands after using the toilet.

Symptoms: Flulike symptoms, nausea, vomiting, loss of appetite, aches, tenderness in right upper abdomen, jaundice, malaise.

Prognosis: Long illness.

Cure/Treatment: Rest, sometimes for weeks, and healthy diet.

Warning: If allowed to continue, hepatitis A can lead to liver failure and other complications, including coma and death.

---

[26]Known in Latin as a *titus*.
[27]Known as the *hep*.

Hepatitis B

Other names: Kissing disease; needle-sharing-junkie's disease, sloppy-tattoo-"artist"-in-Manila disease.

Locale: Human habitations.

Cause: Sexual contact; use of unsterilized needles for ear piercing, tattooing, or drug injection.

Prevention: Vaccine for people at especially high risk; immunoglobulins.

Symptoms: Same as hepatitis A.

Prognosis: Years of usually low-grade illness.

Cure/Treatment: None.

Warning: Can lead to cirrhosis of the liver and liver cancer. Infected (contagious) victims may show no symptoms.

Malaria

Names: Four different protozoan organisms, the worst being *Plasmodium falciparum.*

Locale: Warm, damp places.

Cause: Bite of female anopheles mosquito.

Prevention: At night in a malarial area, stay indoors and wear long-sleeved shirts, long pants, and potent insect repellent. Malaria can sometimes be prevented by taking chloroquine phosphate one week before the trip and for six weeks afterward.

Symptoms: Onset may occur in a week or not for a year if antimalarial drugs are used. First signs are severe headache and fever, sometimes to 105° F. Bouts of shaking, chills, and profuse sweating may appear every two or three days. *Plasmodium falciparum* can cause anemia, convulsions, kidney and liver failure, coma, and death within hours.

Prognosis: Can become chronic.

Cure/Treatment: In extreme cases, a complete blood exchange may be the only way to save a life.

Warning: Malaria is a medical emergency requiring an immediate trip to the hospital.

Rabies

Other names: Hydrophobia (fear of water); Cujomouth, vicious-looking-skunk-in-the-yard.

Locale: Check your local listings or call the police or ASPCA.

Cause: Bite or lick from infected mammal, causing an acute viral infection of the nervous system. In Asia, dogs are the most common carriers; in Russia, wolves; in Africa, jackals; in South America, bats; in North America, skunks and raccoons.

Prevention: Vaccination for those in high-risk jobs, such as animal control officers and employees of George Steinbrenner. Avoid people and animals that act strange and/or froth at the mouth. Animals that are normally nocturnal may appear during the day if infected. Rabid animals often look like they're trying to say something important, like "Damien! Damien! It's all for you, Damien!"

Symptoms: Hyperactivity, disorientation, delirium, paralysis of eye and facial muscles, seizures. Constriction and spasms of throat muscles can make swallowing difficult or impossible despite intense thirst. Coma and death occur within three weeks of onset.

Prognosis: Almost always fatal without prompt treatment. A few victims have survived with the help of machinery to keep their hearts and lungs working. Prayer and folk medicine are fine as accompaniments to treatment in a modern hospital setting.

Cure/Treatment: Human rabies immunoglobulin treatments begun within two days and continuing for several weeks almost always cure the disease.

Warning: Do not sew up a bite from an animal that may be rabid. Do not become overly excited. Try to capture or kill the offending animal for examination, but do not shoot it in the head, as its brain will be needed to test for rabies.

Yellow Fever

Other names: Plenty-trouble-now.

Locale: Tropical regions.

Cause: Bite of virus-carrying female *Aedes aegypti* mosquito, especially in forest and urban areas of Africa and Central and South America.

Prevention: Vaccination can confer immunity for ten years. Squishing mosquitoes can help alleviate fear and frustration.

Symptoms: Jaundice[28] sets in within three to six days, accompanied by fever, headache, nausea, nosebleeds, and sometimes a slow pulse.

Prognosis: Recovery normally takes three days, but some cases lead to higher fever, severe neck and back pain, and damage to kidney and liver.

Cure/Treatment: No cure is available. Doctors will try to maintain blood volume, sometimes with transfusions.

Warning: Yellow fever is fatal to about 10 percent of victims. The other 90 percent wish they were dead.

SCUBA THRILLS: RUPTURE OF THE DEEP

Kayaking in the jungle isn't the only way to get wet, sick, or killed. There is also scuba diving, a deceptively dangerous sport practiced in beautiful tropical resort areas where nothing could possibly go wrong.

The main problem with scuba diving is that you have to strap a bomb on your back and attach one end to your mouth. A scuba tank is a container stuffed with a whole bunch of air that wants very

---

[28]A medical term meaning "kinda yellowish in color."

ARCHETYPE PROFILE:
ACE SCUBA DIVER

Appearance: Paunchy, tanned,
  grinning.
Home: Miami Beach, Florida.
House: Bungalow near beach.
Employment: Owner of scuba
  magazine.
Vehicle: Custom van.
Preferred Mode of Travel: Free.
Ideal Date: Free crab dinner with
  Polynesian resort owner and several
  of his attractive, extremely friendly
  Polynesian employees.
Worst Fear: Actual work.

---

badly to expand suddenly. Breathing from it underwater, your body becomes another container stuffed
with a whole bunch of air, the difference being that
you are not made of welded steel.

Every thirty-two feet deeper you dive, you add
another lungful of air to lungs that are already full.
If you were to be startled by, say, a ten-foot moray
eel sixty-five feet deep and you bolted for the surface holding your breath, the air in your lungs
would expand to three times the size of your lungs,
but your rib cage would keep them from ballooning
out to Orson Welles proportions. The air would try

to escape through your guts, which would be mighty, mighty unpleasant.

Bubbles could enter your bloodstream, pass through your heart, and end up in the capillaries of your brain, creating a blockage, or embolus, depriving random brain areas of blood. Your IQ could drop permanently to Melanie Griffith levels.

There are other hazards associated with being buried under tons of water. Communication is difficult, for one. Screaming for help works only over short distances, such as those less than six inches. Any other communication must be accomplished with hand signals. Facial expressions are limited because your face is partly covered by a mask and you have a big piece of plastic stuck in your mouth. The only thing you can convey with facial expression alone is wretched terror.[29]

Mouth-to-mouth and cardiopulmonary resuscitation are impossible underwater.

Then there is the problem of the bends.

Because you're inhaling compressed air to match your body's compression underwater, the air in your blood is compressed, like the carbon dioxide in corked champagne.

If you dive too deep for too long and come up too quickly, your blood's capacity to release the compressed air is overwhelmed and bubbles form, just as they do when you open a bottle of champagne.

These noncelebratory bubbles can lodge anywhere but typically get stuck in your joints, your

---

[29]By making your eyes bulge out.

spinal column, and, of course, your brain. The pain sometimes causes victims to double over; thus the name. This is one reason[30] that divers wear expensive watches—to time their rate of ascent and avoid the bends.

The only relief from the bends is to recompress inside a recompression chamber, which is a combination giant scuba tank and tomb. A good recompression chamber has room for a patient, a doctor, and a priest. Once bubbles have cut off the blood supply to portions of your body for more than a few minutes, those portions tend to die off. Recompression will dissolve the bubbles but can't bring flesh back from the dead.

All scuba diving hazards can be minimized by studying the sport for dozens of hours in a classroom setting and practicing repeatedly in controlled environments like swimming pools.

Scuba-diving hazards can be maximized by relying on deeply tanned, sex-crazed, dope-addled "instructors" at cheeseball resorts outside the jurisdiction of American personal injury attorneys.

Learning to Dive with Lance at Club Squid

Diving is like driving—it's perfectly safe if nothing goes wrong and potentially lethal if something does. Experts remain calm and capable in a crisis because they know what to do. Novices, in their ignorance, panic and do the wrong things.

---

[30]Besides looking cool.

If a beach boy we'll call Lance proposes to teach you to scuba dive but is not licensed as an instructor by one of two major diving organizations, the National Association of Underwater Instructors (NAUI) or the Professional Association of Diving Instructors (PADI), ask yourself a few questions:

- Why does Lance live at a seaside resort? Because he is a serious fellow who loves teaching? Or because he loves applying suntan oil to the bodies of adventurous young women from Finland?

- Why is Lance's hair so terribly askew? Was he up all night partying? If he forgets to comb his own hair, will he pay close attention to a non-Scandinavian tourist like you?

- Why doesn't Lance get a real job? A diligent, detail-oriented person—the kind you want as a scuba instructor—would be *managing* the hotel, not hanging out on the dock.

- Is there an extradition treaty between the United States and the country you're in? Can you or your heirs bring Lance to justice if you are injured or killed by Lance's negligence, incompetence, or indifference?

If you want to learn to dive, do it right and in your hometown. Forty hours of training is not too much to prepare for such a complicated and dangerous sport, but it would be a waste of a week's vacation.

Why your survivors should sue Lance and Club Squid. An unlicensed scuba instructor like Lance is probably a free spirit with few possessions—three T-shirts, two pairs of shorts, one pair of thongs, a quarter ounce of decent weed, a pack of rolling papers, and a valid passport. He may also own a plane ticket and may evaporate if you become injured or deceased while enjoying one of his diving excursions.

Lance's parents may be rich, but attaching their assets will be difficult under the best of circumstances, especially if Lance is over eighteen years old.

You might as well go after Lance, just in case. He may have a trust fund. But the assets that can't get away are *those owned by the hotel.* Club Squid has a physical plant and cash flow that can help provide for your survivors.

The resort will probably claim it had nothing to do with Lance, that it never employed him or even knew he had entered the hotel grounds. Local law will prevail, of course, but local authorities won't want bad publicity because they rely so heavily on tourism. If you make a big enough stink, the hotel or the owners' association will pay up.

If they can't pay in cash, maybe they will provide free accommodations for your family and friends on an annual basis, perhaps even during the high season.

Fun 'n' Death at Two Hundred Feet

About three-quarters of the air you breathe is nitrogen, a nontoxic gas. Normally oxygen passes into your bloodstream and nitrogen doesn't, thanks to the design of your lungs. When you breathe air under pressure, however, nitrogen does pass into your bloodstream, creating an effect not unlike inhaling nitrous oxide at the dentist's office.

Dentists give you nitrous when they're going to hurt you more than usual. Once you've taken a few deep breaths of the stuff, your smile becomes broad, which is of incidental benefit to the dentist, who needs room between your lips to insert cotton wads, steel blades, clamps, pumps, and motors.

On nitrous you'll let your dentist do things you'd normally have to be tied down for. They still hurt, but *you simply do not care.* If the dentist decided to scrape tartar off your eyeballs with an old Swiss Army knife, you'd have no objections because nitrous oxide is a beautiful, beautiful thing.

That kind of attitude is fine for gum surgery but can be risky when you're diving. Martini's law states that every fifty feet of depth equals about one martini's worth of bad judgment. At one hundred feet you feel light-headed and may begin giggling. At 150 feet you lose basic motor skills and begin speaking French. At 200 feet you go beyond idiocy and become a menace.

Somewhere deep in the recesses of your brain you know that fish cannot speak and that you cannot breathe water no matter what a bumphead wrasse might tell you. But *you simply do not care.*

This potentially fatal giddiness is known as *nitrogen narcosis,* or rapture of the deep.

You should not go below a hundred feet without a partner or guide who has gone that deep before and lived, preferably a calm dentist-type person who is opposed to silliness.

Don't dive below 135 feet without a very good reason such as (a) you can't stand living anymore or (b) someone's paying you a great deal of money to do it.

Calculating Scuba Safety

To determine the probability of your getting paralyzed or killed on a given scuba dive, use the following equation, where f stands for the depth of the dive in feet; n the number of divers per guide; s your guide's proficiency in a language you speak, in percent; y the number of years before your guide will turn thirty-five; a the total number of alcoholic drinks and marijuana cigarettes you and your guide have consumed in the last three hours; P the hundreds of miles to the nearest recompression chamber; L the hundreds of miles beyond the jurisdiction of your personal negligence attorney; E the total number of dives you have made in your life; and C your honest estimate of your mental age, in years.

$$\frac{\frac{f}{10} + n^3 + \left(\frac{33}{s}\right)^y + 16a + \frac{P+L}{2}}{E + (C - 10)} = \text{probability of grave injury}[31]$$

[31] Tough guys: multiply your final score by 2.

OCEAN MEDICINE

One kind of fish kills far more people than all other sea creatures put together, and it's found in warm, shallow waters all over the world: the ray. A few individuals can survive even in New Jersey waters long enough to sting the crap out of you.

Rays hid under the sand for hundreds of millions of years before we decided to walk into the ocean. They don't expect to be stepped on, so they assume we're trying to eat them; the many species equipped with spines will lash out at you. These stingers have barbs on their barbs and a liberal coating of poison.

A ray may stick its barb into you, where it will break off. Only a surgeon can remove it without ripping a big hole. A ray may simply slash you with the spine; the poison will prevent the wound from healing, which can lead to a serious infection, nasty scarring, and death.

Getting stung by a ray hurts beyond your wildest imagination. Ammonia and household bleach may reduce the pain. Urine is said to contain enough ammonia to lessen the pain but peeing on open wounds is generally a lousy idea. See a doctor.

As for other pain-inflicting sea creatures, what you can expect depends on which ocean you're in.

The Pacific

No matter where you enter the rich waters of the South Pacific, you're likely to be a long way from medical attention. Use the guide below until a doctor or mortician can be found.

The Atlantic and the Caribbean

The Atlantic and Caribbean have few exciting species. Oceangoing cobras, invisible killer jellyfish, saltwater crocodiles, cone-shell mollusks, and heavily armed psychotic Asian pirates may thrive in the Pacific, but they can't survive the pollution in Atlantic waters. When Atlantic seawater gets on somebody's skin or, God forbid, in somebody's eyes or mouth, seek medical attention immediately. Keep the victim warm and dry. Do not induce vomiting or administer alcoholic beverages.

PACIFIC

SYMPTOMS	CAUSE	PROGNOSIS	RESPONSE
Abdominal rigidity, convulsions, paralysis	Sea snake bite	Grim	Keep victim warm and dry; have lawyer draw up will.
Grimacing, convulsions, paralysis	Stonefish sting	Death in minutes	Ask if victim has any final words.

SYMPTOMS	CAUSE	PROGNOSIS	RESPONSE
Purple welts, convulsions, paralysis	Box jelly sting	Death in seconds	Ask if victim has any final gut-wrenching screams.
Limbs torn off at joints	Crocodile attack	End of ballroom dancing career	Shoo away croc; remove victim from water.
Twenty-pound hunk of flesh sheared away	Shark attack	Closed coffin	No more diving until sharks calm down.

ATLANTIC AND CARIBBEAN

SYMPTOMS	CAUSE	PROGNOSIS	RESPONSE
Nausea, diarrhea, dehydration	Exposure to raw sewage	Will live but may not want to	Administer a round of multiple antibiotics.
Night sweats, sudden weight loss, rare cancers	Prick from used hypo-dermic "surf needle"	Death within a decade	Sign victim up for double-blind drug study.

Continued

SYMPTOMS	CAUSE	PROGNOSIS	RESPONSE
Angry rashes, convulsions, dementia	Pesticides flushed into ocean from farmland	Chronic problems with physical and mental health	Sign victim up for long-term care in an institution.
Deep "hash marks" sliced into flesh	Encounter with drunk power-boater	Poor	Stanch bleeding if possible; get boat number.
Broken neck	Cocaine bale dropped from passing aircraft	Highly perky funeral party	Make a trip to Bahamas to open new savings account.
Learning disability, drooling, dementia	Mercury or lead poisoning from flesh of tuna, swordfish, etc.	Chronic mental problems, goog-goog-googly eyes	Eat fewer pelagic fish, more cows and chickens.

SURF AND/OR DIE

Objective comparisons of sports lead to an inescapable conclusion: *nothing could be cooler than surfing a big wave*. It takes years of practice, superb physical condition, big talent, and *huevos grandes*.

Like hang gliders, surfers must sense nature's complex, invisible forces, but a surfer relies on only one simple piece of equipment. Riding a big wave requires balance as fine as any rock or ice climb but adds the element of speed. Surfing is as graceful as skiing but offers more ways to die. It usually

---

ARCHETYPE PROFILE: SURFER ACE

Appearance: Bleached hair, twenty-nine-inch waist, thirty-six-inch chest.

Home: Santa Cruz, California.

House: Three-bedroom ranch with living room telescope and view of Monterey Bay.

Favorite Clothing: Shorts, shark tooth on leather thong.

Vehicle: Cherry '73 International Harvester with mag wheels.

Employment: Dermatologist.

Goal: Acquisition of eighty-foot catamaran.

Worst Fear: Missing a big set.

GLOSSARY FOR
BIG-WAVE WANNABES

aggro ....serious, aggressive

amakua ....spirit guardian

Backdoor..........................North Shore area

brah...brother

caught inside ....caught between breaking
waves and shore

cloudbreak.......huge wave; also Fiji surf spot

da kine ....superior, top-quality

the Duke ....father of modern surfing

the falls..............the breaking part of a wave

foff ....exceptionally fine
(especially referring to women)

foof...........................sound of surfer being
swallowed by a big wave

grommet ....young surf troglodyte

gun ....long board

haole........Caucasian (pronounced "howlie")

harsh on ....criticize

huge ....twenty feet plus

left.........wave breaking to the left as seen by
the rider

North Shore......of Oahu; some of the world's best surfing

pakalolo........Hawaiian sinsemilla, almost as strong as LSD

Pipeline......................North Shore area

rhino chaser..............................long board

sack...*huevos*

set.....................................a wave cycle

skeg...fin

somewhat sizable......................fifteen-foot

stand-up tube..................somewhat sizable hollow wave

stupid...extremely

thruster........................three-skegged board

Waikiki...................................totally bogus

involves sandy beaches. It is essentially free. It can be done naked.

Many big-wave surfers build their lives around the ocean. They drive vehicles big enough to carry a selection of boards. They live near, or even within sight of, waves. Work, sex, families, serious injury, and taxes are mere distractions.

Surfing holds many dangers. The tide can wear you out until you lose your ability to get back to land. The ocean hides boulders and coral heads for

SUAVE-MATIC QUICK REFERENCE GUIDE: SURF SPEAK

STATEMENT	MEANING
This haole had some sack, standing tall inside a dubious barrel over the inside section at Backdoor—and without his ten-foot rhino chaser.	We were impressed with the white man as he rode his small, unstable surfboard inside a huge, irregular wave on the North Shore of Oahu.
The grommets on the beach were harshing on him when he goes over the falls and is under for like three sets before he bobs up with blood pouring out of his ears and a stupid chunk of coral in his mouth.	Surf children were criticizing whitey, despite his daring, when he fell into the wave and was underwater for several minutes before emerging with a severe skull fracture and a need for orthodontia.
When he came to a month later he was totally fine—he still has six teeth and partial sight in one eye. We realized he had an amakua watching over him, so we made him an honorary North Shore brah.	The honky's injuries turned out to be relatively minor. Given his luck and bravery, we decided to speak to him as if he were a human being and not an invader or oppressor.

you to find with your falling body. Big waves can hold you underwater for what seems like—and sometimes is—an eternity. To ride that power and become a part of it means experiencing the dream of living life to its fullest, unifying the eternal and the moment, and possibly getting laid.

You can't learn to surf by reading a book any more than you can learn Zen by watching tennis, but you can learn a few key phrases so people who don't surf will think *you* might be a big-wave surfer.

The Perfect Wave

Waves form in a complicated blend of distant storms, local wind conditions, gravity waves coming off the moon, currents, thermoclines, sea-floor features, and prayer. Waves, rolling tubes of water, can travel thousands of miles before they rise up and break in shallow water, holding human bodies underwater for long periods just for the fun of it.

Surfers search the world looking for waves that break cleanly and are slightly bigger than anything they've ridden before. A clean wave, one with a smooth surface, is the most predictable. Wind that blows too hard can deform waves. Onshore winds, blowing behind a wave, can knock it down. A gentle offshore wind, blowing into the face of a wave, can help hold it up and keep it smooth.

But no wave can truly be perfect without a rider, and no ride can truly be perfect unless everybody sees it. Unfortunately, surfing, like many other dangerous sports, is essentially solitary.

While other people may be on the water or on-shore, few, if any, will be able to see the greatest ride of someone's life. Many surfers want people to see their supreme rides—they want the world to know how inordinately suave they are.

SURF TATTOO DOS AND DON'TS

YES	NO
Maori design	Laura Ashley design
any reptile	any kitten or bunny
shark or barracuda	bass or trout
"Harley-Davidson"	"Kawasaki"
"U.S. Marines"	"Merrill Lynch"
any Archie (except Mr. Whipple)	any Brady (except Jan)
Hawaiian phrase	French phrase
Rastafarian	Republican
Taoist yin-yang symbol	hundred-dollar bill
name of favorite woman	name of favorite town in Ohio

If you want to make a surfer love you forever and die happy, take his[32] picture looking bored inside a big peristaltic ice-blue tube about to slam shut or, arms outstretched, scorching down the black face of some double-overhead monster about to break and snap his board and body in half.

Most surfers, because they are human beings subject to human weaknesses, want to grasp the untouchable and to have a (photographic) record of their moment of perfection, which they can blow up to life size and glue to the ceiling above their bed and frame and hang in their favorite surf shops and make into Christmas cards they can send to their mom and all of their old girlfriends and high school rivals and paint on every billboard from Santa Cruz to San Diego and celebrate in TV commercials on every channel every eight minutes every night for the next twenty or thirty decades.[33]

---

[32]Few women are so grasping and foolish that they need a full-color poster-size photo of themselves surfing a thirty-foot wave littered with broken boards and with a big hammerhead sticking out of it. An eight-by-ten glossy is usually enough for them.

[33]This is not to suggest that surfers are egotistical. It's just that, because surfing is mostly solitary, only a surfer knows how cool he really is, and he wants to be generous and share it with the rest of us.

Your Flavor and the Great White Shark

Drowned surfers outnumber those bitten by sharks by hundreds to one. Still, it's fun to think about Buick-size man-eaters while you're paddling alone, at dusk, half a mile offshore, without an explosive-tipped harpoon.

Most perpetrators are tiger sharks or great whites, usually what scientists call "large individuals," fifteen feet and longer. Ichthyologists have three theories about why sharks sometimes bite surfers:

1. Lying on a board and paddling the California coast, a surfer looks something like an elephant seal from below. Great whites relish fat, juicy elephant seals.

2. Tigers and great whites, like many surfers, are territorial. They don't like to share their waves with anyone.

3. Tigers and great whites are mean motherfuckers.

The most effective shark protection is to take up a different hobby, like Ping-Pong or bassoon.

If you feel you must be in the water and you encounter sharks bigger than you are, pay close attention. If they're swimming rapidly, arching their backs, shuddering, or feeding on other surfers, leave the area.

Some experts recommend striking an attacking shark in the tender regions of the gills or snout. That is about as likely to discourage a shark as threatening it with legal action, but it will give you something to do while your body is shredded into crab bait.

The bright side of shark attacks is that the fish rarely take more than one bite of a human being. Apparently the flavor is all wrong. Few surfers have the layer of blubber sharks expect when biting into a seal. Or maybe it's the body hair—sharks may hate getting it stuck in their teeth. Sometimes they only chew for a minute, without biting clean through, leaving a scar collection that will require hundreds of stitches and impress anyone.

A clean-through bite from a fifteen-footer may cost you twenty pounds of vital organs, but there's no need to worry about it because the shock will kill you more or less instantly. Plus you'll make news around the United States—people love to read about shark attacks—and you'll win a solid reputation as someone intense enough to battle a monster shark to ride a wave.[34]

---

[34]For a shark attack to make news in Australia, it must be fatal and in some way unusual. The victim could be dining in a popular seaside restaurant with several small children, for example, when a sixteen-foot mako leaps out of the water, crashes through a plate-glass window, bites the diner's entire body off at the ankles, and rolls back into the ocean, leaving only a trail of blood, a pair of Tevas, a pair of feet, and three motherless children with no money to pay the breakfast bill.

TOTALLY AT SEA

ARCHETYPE PROFILE: ACE SAILOR

Home: Marblehead, Massachusetts.
House: Five-bedroom Tudor.
Education: Stanford BA, Harvard MBA.
Occupation: Running one of the family firms.
Goal: 'Round the world in eighty days, solo.
Ideal Date: Sharing soda crackers with three-legged Jack Ross dog named Bunny while watching the sun set over Madagascar.
Worst Fear: Losing to an Italian skipper.

Surfing and sailing occupy opposite ends of the sporting expense chart, but they both feature drowning as regular consequences. Sailors also share perspectives with mountaineers. The Mariana Trench, dropping to a crushing world-record depth of more than 36,000 feet in the Pacific Ocean, is 25 percent deeper than Mount Everest is tall, 29,000 feet. Open ocean sailing resembles high-altitude mountaineering in several ways:

• It can get dark.

• It can get cold.

- It can get windy.

- If you get killed, your body may be eaten
  by birds.[35]

Blue-water sailors, like mountain climbers, sometimes have to face nature in her cherished role as the Biggest Cruelest Most Utterly Implacable Ex-Wife from Hell.

If the weather gets bad enough, no one can help a foundering boat or rescue the people on board. No other boat can get close enough to provide assistance; no helicopter can fly steadily enough to pick up survivors.

And weather isn't the only thing that imperils sailors. The human[36] element can be as deadly as a hurricane.

For many open-ocean sailors, of course, the dangers are far outweighed by the rewards—solitude, for example, silence, impossibly starry nights, fellowship, excitement. Commerce, glory, the discovery of new continents or at least an island with guano deposits—these are among the historic joys of sailing.

Ocean sailing is open to anyone who can easily spare $25,000 the first year and at least $5,000 every year thereafter to pour into a bottomless fiberglass pit until it sinks or some other poor sucker buys it.

Becoming a suave ocean sailor can take three

---

[35]Starting with your eyeballs.
[36]Bozo.

generations or more. Portuguese blood is helpful. One must become not only fluent in several difficult languages but a poet and commander in those languages as well. You have to know a Nimrod from a Sea King, a collier from a ketch, T&E from P&L, a #4 mews'l from a #9 spews'l, a port mizz'nj'bs'cle from a f'red'ck'clea'tlshr'd'spr'tpr'tzl, and so on. You have to memorize hundreds of thousands of old sayings, such as

"Pounding headache from Irish sun overhead,
 sailor go right to bed."
"Rosy little balls of fluff at dusk, sailor sure to slap
 on some musk."
"Westerly waves look like Susan Sarandon, sailor
 been alone too long."

While sailors learn their terminology and myth, they should also exercise their imaginations by running mental movies of themselves in every possible sailing disaster.

Favorite Open-Ocean Disasters

People often regret watching their favorite yachts sink. Expense is the least concern, particularly today, what with our advanced methods of insurance. It's sad to see boats sink because they have characters, if not actual souls. It isn't too much to say some people love their boats. Sailors name vessels, share the waves with them, and bid them *dernier voyage* only with deep remorse.

THINGS THAT WILL HURT YOU: SAILBOAT[37]

boom (perfect for fracturing skulls)

shrouds (hang up on things and drag them down as the boat sinks)

keel (breaks off, causing you to lose steering ability)

cleats (stub your toe so badly on them you'll want to sue somebody)

batteries (squirt acid, go dead)

stove (starts a fire)

signal flares (start a fire)

propane tank (high explosive)

deck (slippery)

height of gunwale (can make it impossible to get back into the boat without help)

draft (hits bottom, causing loss of boat and contents)

motor (seizes up at the wrong moment)

propeller (chops you up)

exhaust pipe (rusts through and lets water into the bilge)

bilge pump (will definitely fail; the question is when)

mast (falls and splits your skull open like a melon)

hull (fragile when up against coral, rocks, submerged logs, or killer whales)

skipper (makes bad judgments)

crew (follows skipper's dumb orders)

---

[37]Partial list.

Of course there is the question of honor. No one likes to be considered a poor sailor.

Finally, skippers, crew, and passengers alike prefer to be in boats rather than nostril-deep in a bellowing gale and steep seas in the middle of the night a thousand miles downwind of the nearest land.

Insurance can mitigate financial pain; blame can be placed on impossible-to-foresee events or on jelly-witted persons of no blood relation to the one telling the story. A loss of hands, however, will spoil a holiday like nothing else, and no amount of explaining will satisfy the survivors.

The causes of boating losses fall into three categories: skipper error, nonskipper error due to skipper error, and nonskipper error compounded by skipper error. Entire volumes have been written on imaginative ways to sink a boat; there is room here to outline only the most common.

Faulty Weather Prediction. Even experienced sailors sometimes believe weather reports issued by a major government agency or an alleged meteorologist named Windy or Storm. These agencies and reporters never disclose that they are no better at predicting what the weather will be like three days from now than a family of raccoons. Many meteorologists think weather prediction is a kind of guessing game where losers get caught in the rain without umbrellas. Ha-ha!

Parading around the studio in their helmetlike hairdos, heavy makeup, and fancy clothes, these "journalists" seem unaware that crabs are battling eels for the right to consume some ex-viewer's internal organs in total darkness six thousand feet deep on the ocean floor.

Sailors intending to stray more than three hours[38] from port should always be prepared to ride out a typhoon and should stay tuned to weather reports. These reports are sometimes accurate at predicting weather up to three *hours* in advance.

Faulty Navigation. The declining cost and increasing accuracy of loran and other electronic positioning systems are giving more sailors a chance to find out exactly where they are when they run aground.

Even with an accurate fix, accurate charts, and a firm grasp of local tides, many skilled sailors hit bottom because they don't have a realistic idea of how much progress they can make in shallow waters before the tide turns.

Additionally, no chart reveals every rock and coral head. If one of the world's most skilled pilots can run the *Queen Elizabeth II* aground, no weekend Ahab should feel too confident about shallow-water navigation.

Equipment Failure. Mike Plant, one of the world's best single-handed sailors, was killed not long ago, possibly because he failed to think carefully about the way his ballast bulb was screwed to the tip of his keel. It may have snapped off suddenly, causing his fancy racing boat, *Coyote*, to flip so quickly he was knocked unconscious and drowned. It may have struck a whale or a submerged tree trunk or even a

---

[38]Remember the tragic tale of the *Minnow*, lost on what was meant to be a three-hour tour, *a three-hour tour.*

submarine. Before you laugh, ask yourself how many times a year you think carefully about *your* ballast bulb bracket bolts.

The relentless motion of the sea eventually works loose every bolt, weld, and knot and every glued, nailed, and stapled thing on a boat.

Salt water has intensely corrosive powers, especially on metal objects such as exhaust pipes, radios, batteries, electrical wiring, sockets, pumps, cleats, shrouds, rivets, welds, masts, footings, and tools. Small critters in salt water, such as gribbles and marine worms, are happy to drill into wood, even treated wood, until it is eaten away or almost invisibly softened to the consistency of a foam mattress.

Just like living things, all vital equipment is mortal. The sea has a final claim on every piece of it and on every boat. The question is not whether the sea will make good on those claims but when.

With this in mind, imaginative open water sailors have a life raft on board—stored on the *outside* of the boat—and an abandon-ship bag close by. The abandon-ship bag should include at least one passport and half a gallon of water per person, a mini-EPIRB,[39] a VHF radio, fishing equipment, soy sauce and pickled ginger, floppy hats, a paperback copy of *Jaws*, the twenty-third psalm printed on a waterproof card, suntan lotion, at least one Game

---

[39]If you think someone will get your EPIRB (Emergency Position-Indicating Radio Beacon) signal and rescue you, take ten deep breaths and try to get a grip on reality. The Coast Guard looks into about 2.8 percent of EPIRB alarms. They are too busy failing to catch dope smugglers to help people who are actually in trouble.

Boy, and cyanide tablets for when the Game Boy batteries die.

Collision. Understanding the rules of the sea will help you avoid collisions. The boat on the starboard tack[40] is normally the privileged vessel, the one with the right-of-way. The numerous exceptions to this rule include the following: the other boat is a commercial or fishing vessel; the other boat is a larger or smaller vessel; the other skipper is trying to impress a passenger or is distracted by a glimpse of an excellent tan line on a passenger's body; the other skipper got out on the wrong side of the bunk this morning; the other skipper has been drinking heavily all day; the other skipper never bothered to study the rules of the sea; visibility is too poor for anyone to see you until it's too late.

A single long blast of your horn means "I intend to leave you on my port side, you son of a mongrel."

Fire or Explosion. Most flammable and explosive materials should be kept on land. Nevertheless, boatbuilders, in the interest of high-seas adventure, traditionally incorporate flammable materials into yacht construction, including wood, paint, varnish, and the resins that hold fiberglass together. Sailors add gasoline or diesel fuel, lubricating oils, hydraulic fluids, and propane used for cooking. Throw in some oily rags, old ropes, a small library of trashy novels and pornography, a can of bacon grease, and a few yards of sculpted shag carpet, and you can burn an entire yacht to the water line in minutes.

---

[40]That's the boat on the right.

TEAR-OUT SKIPPER PRIORITY LISTS

Which of these priority lists most closely resembles your own? Tear it out of the book[41] and paste it near the helm.

SKIPPER PRIORITIES, OLD-SCHOOL DIVISION

1. safety of paying passengers
2. safety of crew
3. safety of those on other vessels
4. own safety
5. own vessel
6. other vessels
7. vital equipment
8. honor

SKIPPER PRIORITIES, LIFE-IS-SHORT DIVISION

1. getting laid
2. looking cool
3. par-TAAAAAAY!
4. nice weather

SKIPPER PRIORITIES, MONACO BERTH DIVISION

1. having largest boat in class
2. having most expensive boat in class
3. having fastest boat in class
4. hot-looking babes

---

[41]After you pay for it.

SKIPPER PRIORITIES, RACING DIVISION

1. winning
2. placing second
3. placing third
4. hot-looking babes

At a distance, a fire like that might remind you of Elizabeth, New Jersey. Up close, one whiff of the smoke can knock you unconscious; the second whiff can be fatal.

A common sailing mistake starts with a vague smell of something burning, perhaps in the engine compartment. As the curious and mildly concerned sailor opens the compartment door, air rushes in and turns a previously smoldering fire into a blast furnace, burning off all of the sailor's hair and ruining a perfectly good vacation.

Fire may kill all electrical systems and make a Mayday impossible. The advantage of fire is that billowing black smoke may summon other vessels in time to pluck survivors from the water.

Person[42] Overboard. Falling off a boat is dangerous chiefly because a human head is hard to see at a distance, especially in rough seas. Whoever sees an

---

[42]Known according to ancient tradition as a "man" and thus internationally recognized by the sexist acronym MOB.

SAILING TERMINOLOGY QUIZ

Think you're a sailor? How many of the following terms can you identify?

1. **fo'c'sle:** (a) upper deck between foremast and bow; (b) foxhole; (c) type of lewd Popsicle; (d) all of the above
2. **forefoot:** (a) where stem and keel meet; (b) leading tine of a cleat; (c) part of clam dipped in melted butter; (d) all of the above
3. **hellosailer:** (a) hail from skipper to shore; (b) hail from shore to skipper; (c) hail from whore to skipper; (d) crab louse
4. **Maccallan:** (a) three-masted schooner; (b) single-malt Scotch; (c) star of *Dune*, "Twin Peaks," and *Blue Velvet*; (d) all of the above
5. **reef:** (a) reduce sail area; (b) part of a sail taken in or let out; (c) something to smash into; (d) all of the above
6. **roach:** (a) curve of sail; (b) galley insect; (c) grounds for search and seizure of vessel in territorial waters of the United States; (d) all of the above
7. **strake:** (a) band of hull planking; (b) frigate bird; (c) work stoppage by Irish crew members; (d) all of the above
8. **Thorshavn:** (a) Icelandic port; (b) Faeroe Island port; (c) tawny port; (d) all of the above

9. **warp:** (a) hauling with a rope or cable attached to a fixed object; (b) such a rope or cable; (c) 10 percent of lightspeed; (d) all of the above
10. **yaw:** (a) rising and falling motion; (b) sideways motion; (c) disease of fish; (d) all of the above

Answers: 1. a; 2. a; 3. c; 4. b; 5. d;
6. d; 7. a; 8. b; 9. d; 10. b.

MOB has a single job: as a pair of eyeballs Super Glued to that bobbing head. The witness does not "go find the skipper" or "try to calm down" but instead wails and points at the swimmer until he or she is back on board.

If the MOB appears to be drowning, the MOB will be in a state of extreme panic and may be more dangerous than a mako with a number 12 hook in its mouth. The lifesaver's rule is *throw, tow, row,* and, as a last resort, *go swimming.*

First throw the MOB a life jacket or anything else that floats. If that fails, try throwing a rope or extending a paddle or gaff to the poor swimmer and towing him or her to the boat. If that fails, row or paddle to the MOB on a sailboard or raft. If all of these methods fail, assign someone with martial arts training to swim to the MOB, beat him or her unconscious, and drag him or her back to the boat.

When the victim regains consciousness, provide swimming lessons.

If you lose sight of an MOB, immediately send out an MOB Pan-Pan signal[43] to request assistance with the search.

Sinking. If the hull is ruptured, send a distress signal immediately because incoming water could short your batteries. Do not stuff life jackets in the hole. You may need them.

Do not touch bilge water if any electrical wires may be feeding current into it.

A four-inch hole below the water line will welcome about two hundred gallons a minute into your vessel. Few electric bilge pumps can remove more than sixty gallons a minute from a boat. Not even Arnold can manually pump thirty gallons a minute for more than ten minutes. Deploy life raft.

When you learn a helicopter is en route, deploy checkbook.

Think of something nice to say to your crew, friends, and family, such as "In case we don't make it out of this jam, I want you to know something: I really, really like you."

When the helicopter arrives and sends down a line, do not attach it to your vessel unless you want a large aircraft to crash on top of you.

---

[43]If you don't know what a Pan-Pan signal is, don't assume the role of skipper just yet.

SUAVE-MATIC QUICK REFERENCE GUIDE: SAIL SPEAK

STATEMENT	MEANING
I built her of carvel-planked khaya on oak with extra-heavy scantlings.	I have such an excess of time and money that I insist my mahogany be African.
The breakers were coming across the wave train and carrying us quite a distance on our beam ends.	What I thought was a boat turned out to be a Boogie board.
The halyard and lazyjacks snapped, and the falling yard shattered the pram hood.	A bunch of wood and cables smashed my windshield.
The wing hatch was held shut by the weight of the boom, yard, and custom battens from my vast private collection.	Despite my vast financial resources and superb breeding, I couldn't see a damn thing.
I started the bilge pump.	The water was crotch-deep.

Continued

STATEMENT	MEANING
We were starting to wish we were somewhere else.	The boat and I were kissing each other good-bye.
A banana boat came by at the last minute and hauled me on board.	Can you imagine? Saved by minorities!
They towed her under. I regret not going down with her.	The banana boat skipper was a boob. Am I not a noble fellow in comparison?

SPELUNKER'S GUIDE TO TOTAL DARKNESS

Caving may offer more varieties of unspeakable terror than any other sport. There are your two basic Freudian fears of (a) entering an impossibly deep, impossibly dark, wet hole squirming with blind white animals and (b) getting stuck in that hole forever.

Cavers also face more prosaic fears like being enclosed by billions of tons of rock, getting lost, contracting hypothermia, falling off cliffs, drowning, and accidentally touching bat shit.

Then there is the trip to the cave itself. Many of the best caves are found in alarmingly rural areas where the local people eat, drink, and breathe superstition. Because few residents have college educations, they tend to fear caves and bats and blind white reptiles, which some say are the devil's own critters and a wicked pestilence that ought to be harassed, mutilated, and killed in the name of the loving Lord Jesus.

Besides being a reminder of hell, a cave may

ARCHETYPE PROFILE: ACE SPELUNKER

Appearance: Powerfully built ultrageek.

Home: Riverside, California.

House: Three-bedroom ranch.

Education: Master's in mechanical engineering, Ph.D. in solid-state physics, MIT.

Favorite Clothing: Custom-made dry suit.

Occupation: Systems engineer.

Goal: Making the first Lechuguilla connection.

Current Reading: Heidegger's *Unterwegs zur Sprache*.

Worst Fear: Nothingness.

---

mean tourism to the local people or perhaps a handy place to throw garbage. Local folk don't cotton to strangers coming in and wanting to go down in them caves. What fur? they want to know, and How long you gonna be down in thet hoe? You leave word with any your kin 'bout where you was goin'? You leave any good stuff in yur car?

Rotting garbage or a little gift shop can make a cave entrance seem even more fetid than it is naturally, but rattlesnakes create problems beyond the merely aesthetic. A cave may provide a temperature-controlled refuge for snakes during cold weather, so they may be encountered near the entrance in the spring.

The walls of some cave entrances are steep enough to trap snakes that survive the fall into the pit. These reptiles can be found year-round, often in foul moods. Mixed in with other detritus at the bottom of the entrance, rattlers can be hard to see in the dark. Their bites, while gruesome, are rarely fatal, and once past the entrance area, cavers can forget about venomous reptiles and start thinking about bats.

Bats in a cave are accustomed to such deep silence and darkness that your arrival in their chamber might disturb them and cause them to flit about. Contrary to what a cave entrance gift shop attendant might tell you, they will not get in your hair.

While flitting and squeaking bats cause even some well-educated cavers to shudder and flail their arms, the animals deserve our affection. They are more closely related to voles and shrews than mice or rats. That is comforting, isn't it? They have incredibly soft fur, acute hearing, and prodigious insecticide abilities. One little brown bat can consume six hundred mosquitoes an hour. Ten thousand little brown bats can cause people with mild bat phobias to lose control of their bowels.

As helpful as bats are to us, there is one reason to fear them: like skunks and raccoons, they sometimes carry rabies. If you are bitten by a bat in North America, it is almost certainly rabid, as the range of vampire bats extends no farther north than Colombia. If you're lucky enough to catch the offending creature, do not crush its little skull, because its brain will be needed to check for the presence of rabies.

Compared to other wilderness, of course, caves are notably free of flora and fauna. The excitement of caves derives from their hidden, otherworldly nature. On most other expeditions you can see the quarry. Even if weather blocks your view, you can look at maps and compasses to plot a course. Not so with expedition caving. Virgin caves are secret until someone penetrates them. They remain secret if those who penetrate them never get back out again.

Exploring virgin caverns takes more money, time, experts, and equipment than an assault on Everest. Most big caves are formed by water, so most big caves contain rivers. Unless the members of the expedition team want to lug hundreds of oxygen tanks or a compressor into a wet cave, they have to use rebreathers, self-contained air scrubbing and recycling systems.

You can't just go out and buy rebreathers from

NAME-DROPPER'S NOTES

Huautla, a limestone cave near Oaxaca, Mexico, is one of the biggest unexplored holes in the world.[44] Huautla is almost three thousand feet deep. As you might expect, ancient Aztec hieroglyphs have not been found over a mile into the cave. The Aztecs were not even close to stupid enough to go anywhere near a cave as big and deep as Huautla.

Lechuguilla, a great big cave in California, was formed by sulfuric acids rather than the carbolic acids that formed most other caves. The action of the sulfuric acids has left huge, rare crystal formations, some of them amazingly delicate. Lechuguilla is humid like most other caves, but it's also a relatively warm 68° F.

The fragile nature of the crystal formations allowed serious cavers to convince the government to restrict access to the hole. More than fifty miles of the cave have been mapped by teams blessed with official government permission. The only known entrance, dug by cavers in 1986, is equipped with a locked gate to prevent hapless imbeciles from wandering in, wrecking delicate formations, and getting flatrocked.

---

[44]Second only to downtown Detroit.

your local NASA outlet. NASA isn't selling, and, any-way, its units are crappy—they're too bulky and inefficient. No, if you want to do major caves, you'll have to invent, build, test, and perfect your own rebreathers.

The best rebreathers are slightly bulkier and more delicate than mainframe computers. If your experimental rebreathing unit happens to shut down after, say, a mile-long swim into a cave, you then become an ex-inventor buried in one of the world's deepest graves.

If you're not a brilliant inventor and must breathe old-fashioned compressed air, you have to be able to get back to base before your air runs out. This can be challenging in raging, unmapped un-derground rivers that are at least as dark as the inside of a buried coffin. Failing a return to base, you must find an air pocket and hope someone finds you before you consume the oxygen there.

Serious caving requires long walks while pain-fully hunched over, long crawls on the belly, tight squeezes through tiny cracks and keyholes, and careful climbing on slick surfaces over yawning abysses. To add to the horror, long expeditions re-quire cavers to eat freeze-dried foods. This can lead to uniquely dreadful flatulence, which can remain trapped for days in the room where it is issued. Finally, everyone must carry out his or her sewage, since it would last for centuries in a cave's microbe-poor environment.

If you have the daring, stamina, inventiveness, odor tolerance, time, and money to be a big-time

SUAVE-MATIC QUICK
REFERENCE GUIDE: CAVE SPEAK

STATEMENT	MEANING
We found thirty-foot strands of angel hair in a new lead off Owsley's Esophagus.	We found amazingly long gypsum crystals in a place no creature bigger than a microbe has ever visited.
I had such a nasty case of crystal crotch I had to kind of stagger to keep my thighs from rubbing together.	Sweat and gypsum crystals, combining in my shorts, severely impeded my suavosity.
I was trying to cross a catwalk in this geekoid fashion when I slipped on foot-deep rockflour, pulled a half-ton block off the wall, and went straight into the Void.	Inching across a virgin ledge, I slipped on the excrement of microscopic creatures and fell into the jaws of death accompanied by a rock the size of a steamer trunk.
For about two seconds Annie and I thought I was flatrocked for sure.	Everybody figured I would be splattered like a cartoon coyote.

STATEMENT	MEANING
The slab landed right next to me in an Olympic-size sapphire pool.	Although I soiled the pure waters with my filthy biomass, I felt OK about it.
I Jumarred back up to the catwalk, and we mapped our booty and decided to call it Towering Backflip.	I used special clamps to climb the rope my partner sent down to me; you're now obligated to use our name for the place because we discovered it.

cave explorer, chances are you can find a date on Saturday night. What more could a person want?

Caving fame.

The Holy Grail of caving is to make a "connection"—find another exit[45] and not come out the way you went in. Besides getting lost and drowning in underground rivers, two dangers confront the spelunker: falling and getting stuck, sometimes simultaneously.

---

[45]Other than death.

Broken bones present a problem deep inside a cave, where rescue can be difficult or impossible. Broken limbs jammed into small cracks are worse. Typically a caver gets stuck in such a tight spot that only one person at a time can provide help or comfort. Yanking a body out of a crack is harder than laypeople imagine, even if the body has lost twenty or thirty pounds from hunger and dehydration.

Because many caves are permanently cool, usually in the low fifties, stuck cavers tend to die of exposure. The rock surrounding them absorbs their body heat until they don't have any more.

Every decade or so the public imagination is captured by the story of somebody trapped in a cave. Death from exposure takes long enough to allow TV crews to arrive at the cave entrance and artists' conceptions of the predicament to be drawn for viewers at home. It's a slow-motion disaster. Comments[46] relayed from victim to the public provide extra pathos.

Typically these victims are amateurs and/or fools who entered the cave alone and/or without proper preparation or equipment. The death of a serious caver is, by contrast, expected—it is not exactly a major news story:

HALF MILE INTO FAST-MOVING, 100 PERCENT PITCH-BLACK UNDERGROUND RIVER, CAVE EXPLORER DROWNS
WIFE AND KIDS: "NOT REAL SURPRISED"

---

[46]Usually including last words.

EXTREME WETNESS

Like other dangerous, expensive, glamorous pursuits, expedition caving attracts weird birds and nutjobs. Big-time spelunkers have the same rare combinations of abilities as astronauts:

- They work well in teams and yet are highly self-reliant.

- They can maintain a steady level of wide-eyed, detail-oriented paranoia for days without slipping over into panic even for a moment.

- They secretly enjoy spending entire weekends in extremely cramped quarters with sweaty guys who smell bad.

Extreme Falling

ARCHETYPE PROFILE:
ACE PARACHUTIST

Appearance: Former junior varsity athlete, snappy clothes, subtle comb-over, modest gold chain.

Home: Dayton, Ohio.

House: Subdivision two-bedroom, one-and-a-half-bath.

Vehicle: Chevrolet Corvette.

Occupation: Inside sales.

Goal: Free fall from 120,000 feet while filming himself.

Ideal Date: Asti Spumante and multimedia record of his jump career for favorite waitress.

Worst Fear: Women making fun of him.

WHAT SIZE IS YOUR PARACHUTE?

Airborne events like skydiving and hang gliding offer the polar opposites of caving. Instead of grim, crushing darkness and terror, falling offers grim, sunny, weightless terror.

Caving thrills are grubby and elusive. No event you could expect to survive, on the other hand, could offer more raw excitement than your first skydive. It will knock sex several notches down on your thrill chart. Any sex. With anyone. It's fairly cheap to get started, you can do it in otherwise thrill-free regions such as Indiana, and people who are afraid of flying will be impressed to learn you jumped out of an aircraft on purpose.

As you let go of the plane three thousand feet above the ground, every cell in your body and every fiber of your animal instinct screams scathing epithets at you in unison.

Every gland and biological system prepares for termination. You had been told to count to some number and got to approximately one. You don't feel terror, exactly, because terror is a natural response meant to help you survive. This time your body and nature have given up on you entirely.

You can't even scream.

In a static line jump, you fall four hundred feet before the chute opens with a jolt: the jolt of life itself. No planned thrill can surpass that sweet, pointed, abrupt return to time and space, to the world of the living.

Like junkies, sky divers return to the sky looking for that original thrill, but it wears off until they can actually count down and deploy their own chutes in a free fall. With enough practice they can relax enough to do things besides count while falling, such as perform stunts or, if truly courageous, get married.

Landing, of course, is the most dangerous part of the sport. It's best to be moving forward when you hit the ground, because otherwise you might fall over backward, hit your head, and look dumb. The old World War II–type round chutes have sections missing from the back. Air flows through them out of the chute, giving jumpers about eight miles an hour of forward motion so they don't descend at the whim of the wind. Nobody should use round chutes anymore, but some troglodyte jump schools still have a few lying around. Modern rectangular "air-ram" chutes have sections that channel the air for the same purpose.

Coming down in, say, a twelve-mile-an-hour wind, a jumper, back to the wind, moves horizontally at twenty miles per hour. The vertical speed, meanwhile, is about what you'd reach jumping from ten or twelve feet off the ground. Hitting the ground in a twelve-mile-an-hour wind is thus like jumping from the roof of a school bus moving at twenty miles per hour, just like highly trained Hollywood stuntmen do after they have received a great deal of money.

To make matters worse, jumpers lack perspective on their target[47] as it rises up to slam into them.

---

[47]The ground.

The only way to predict the arrival of the earth is to watch the horizon so you can get a sense of the movement of the entire plane of the ground. Unfortunately, this is counterintuitive. It's hard not to look down at the last moment. With an old-fashioned round chute you'll have to roll when you hit, just like a stuntman jumping off a school bus, to spread the impact out over as wide an area as possible. With a rectangular chute you'll be able to land gently, but only if you know where the ground is.

Although your teachers will tell you you're unlikely to get killed, no one will be at all surprised if you break your leg.

If you attend a jump school approved by the U.S. Parachutists Association (USPA), you won't have to use old-fashioned round chutes. The modern rectangular chutes are so maneuverable that with practice you'll swoop in like a bird and touch down in sneakers as if you're stepping off a curb.

Tandem jumping provides a way to free-fall on your first jump. Make sure your teacher is specially certified in tandem jumping and isn't just trying to get close enough to feel your goose bumps. You'll have your teacher strapped on your back, and he or she will pull the rip cord on the extralarge chute you'll share.

The other modern instructional method, accelerated free fall (AFF), now allows novices to keep themselves more consistently terrified than ever before. Two instructors jump from nine thousand feet while hanging on to you. In the event that you turn pale and allow your tongue to flap in the wind, they are required by USPA rules not to tell anyone. If you are able to remain conscious, they will let you know when to pull your rip cord. If you become incoherent, they will slap you across the face three times before pulling your cord for you.

Note: A few unscrupulous people, many of whom are now deservedly dead, have passed themselves off as AFF and tandem instructors just long enough to get beginners out of the plane, where no one can ask about certification because it's too noisy for conversation. Ask to see certification documents *before deploying your wallet*. Because your life will be on the line, you might inquire as to whether your instructors are full-time jump professionals or if this is just their "neat hobby."

Tree-Slamming Technique

If you're falling out of the sky and into the woods, make a quick assessment of the trees. Are they less than twenty feet tall? The proper technique may seem obvious: try to land between them.

That method is improper in tall trees, however, because your chute may catch on a high branch and deflate, causing you to fall—in this case more than twenty feet. In tall, closely spaced trees you'll have to take a shot at slamming *directly into the tree trunk* and hanging on. Unfortunately, tree trunks hit considerably harder than Mike Tyson.

If you survive that encounter, you may want to take up a career in prizefighting after your postparachute orthodontia.

SUAVE-MATIC QUICK REFERENCE GUIDE: CHUTE SPEAK

STATEMENT	MEANING
Although she was an AFF-rated JM and knew her BSR, she declined a pin check during takeoff.	Despite her official jump master training in basic safety requirements, her ego was too fragile for her to allow anyone to double-check her gear on the plane.
She pulled at under two thousand feet and had a pilot chute in tow, thanks to a twisted leg strap.	With her main chute still in the bag at seventeen hundred feet, she had about six seconds to get her act together.
She tried to pull the main canopy breakaway handle instead of going directly for the reserve.	She was more afraid of both chutes opening and getting tangled than of striking a medium-size planet at high speed.

STATEMENT	MEANING
By the time she pulled her reserve, she was three hundred feet off the DZ.	She needed at least four hundred feet for the reserve chute to open and slow her fall to the drop zone.
She always claimed AADs were for beginners.	An automatic activation device, which would deploy the emergency chute at a preset altitude and speed, would have been a wise investment.
These errors resulted in one of skydiving's rare fatalities.	It took her several hours to die from the massive internal injuries.

Sky Surfing

It isn't just for Reebok ads anymore. People who have jumped out of airplanes several hundred times and find the free fall dull can now complicate matters by trying to free-fall on a honeycombed-aluminum Boogie board.

The sky surfboard does not want to be ridden— it wants to become the blades of a helicopter.

If you've ever tried to deploy a parachute while spinning uncontrollably upside down, consult a psychiatrist.

"Normal" jumpers open their chutes while falling as slowly as possible, with their bodies in a belly-flop position. The successful sky surfer must deploy in a vertical[48] position. Bodies fall much faster when pointed at the ground, which puts more strain on the parachutes, sometimes causing them to explode. Pack a spare.

Death Kite 2000

To prolong the parachute experience, some people with sewing skills and a lot of extra nylon and free time invented the parapente. Paragliding is the closest a human being can come to actual flying without spending the money to go hang gliding. A breeze in the big parapente, a kind of rectangular parachute, can lift you off the ground without relying on an airplane, and the chute is much simpler and more flexible than a hang glider. A parapente requires no airspeed, so you can stall it without getting killed.

Standing on a gentle slope, novice paragliders face the wind, reading its subtleties. When the conditions are right, they run down the slope, filling their nylon wing with air. Launched sideways, they are dragged across the slope by their colorful nylon

---

[48]Preferably upright.

chutes and get badly bruised and humiliated, perhaps losing a couple of front teeth.

Like parachutes, parapentes can be steered
with toggles and stalled for a landing by pulling on
both toggles at once. Skilled pilots of all kinds of
aircraft are able to locate the updrafts known as
thermals, but skilled paragliders make the best of
narrow thermals because parapentes have a turning
radius only slightly wider than a buzzard's.

NAME-DROPPER'S NOTE

The suave paraglider will learn to speak
French because the French Alps are world parapente headquarters. Flying silently from la
mountaintop to le tiny-French-restaurant-in-
the-woods-above-Chamonix, one can experience un high point du civilization.

Your maitre d' may laugh when you show
up wearing a lavender jumpsuit with silver
piping, but the escargots alone will be worth
the embarrassment.

A new parapente costs only a couple of thousand bucks, and it can be carried up a mountain like
a backpack. A hang glider is so unwieldy and complex the pilot needs a trailer just to get the damn
thing down a road. If you plan to climb a hill with
an assembled hang glider, be sure to bring along
three or four powerfully built people to help you.

BASE JUMPING

Certain people think planes are a hassle so they jump from stationary objects like buildings, bridges, and cliffs wearing parachutes. They get killed all the time. On average they have the strongest death wish of all sportspersons who are not already dead.

When a survivor calls a jumper's parents to report their child's death, Mom and Dad usually make comments like "You don't say. Splattered, huh? That's a darn shame."

No cliff big enough to jump from is truly vertical. If you think parachuting into a tree or power line might be messy, imagine hitting a jagged rock face during a free fall.

One trouble with tall buildings[49] is the wind patterns they create. Remember: *you can't see air.* No building is tall enough to allow for second chances or nice things like emergency chutes.

Another problem is that few skyscrapers are surrounded by grassy areas—pavement makes for hard touchdowns.

Wise people who jump from buildings have a fast stolen car waiting for them at the DZ with passenger side door open, the engine running, and a skilled driver at the wheel.

Unlike buildings and cliffs, bridges and cranes don't get in your way once you jump from them. They don't rise far enough off the ground, however,

---

[49]Besides security guards and laws against trespassing.

ARCHETYPE PROFILE:
ACE BASE JUMPER

Appearance: MTV T-shirt, untied high-top basketball shoes, laserlike glare.

Home: Montclair, New Jersey.

House: Owned by parents.

Vehicle: No.

Driver's License: Suspended.

Ideal Date: Receiving oral sex while doing Ecstasy, listening to Mudhoney, watching Monday Night Football, eating pizza, smoking a joint, talking on the phone, and drinking Olde English 800 and tequila shots on a water bed.

Goal: Smoking superior California bud in a clean bong before jumping off the George Washington Bridge at rush hour on 'shrooms while listening to Led Zeppelin on a portable compact disc player and watching a laser light show on virtual reality glasses and then landing on the dance floor of the *Queen Elizabeth II* for a glass of ice-cold Dom Perignon.

Worst Fear: Being like his or her parents.

Second Worst Fear: Having to move out of his or her parents' house.

to allow for the slightest hesitation or delay in deploying a chute. For those who need thrills this big, we recommend shooting a blend of cocaine, heroin, and Listerine. It's almost as thrilling and safer for you and for bystanders.

Jump!

Bungee jumping is essentially a vertical roller coaster ride, not a sporting event. No talent is required of a bungee jumper; no honor is conferred.

It's OK, even desirable, to have consumed mind-altering substances before bungee jumping. Not so with an actual sport like skydiving or hang gliding.

Bungee jumping can be thrilling, but so is Space Mountain at Disneyland. Neither is dangerous. More people get killed masturbating.

No, bungee jumping is not a sport. It isn't even a game, because everybody wins. You wouldn't call people "master bungee jumpers" except to humiliate them. So if you were hoping to read about bungee jumping in this book, forget it.

HANG U.

Great strides have been made since hang gliding was invented in the late sixties by people who had run out of hard drugs. Morticians can do wonders today for families who insist on open caskets, wrenching limbs and torsos back into place until they look remarkably straight and lifelike.

ARCHETYPE PROFILE: ACE HANG GLIDER PILOT

Appearance: Earnest and beefy in a sportshirt, perfectly ironed designer blue jeans, and a gimme cap.

Home: Glendale, California.

House: Ranch with moldy aboveground pool out back.

Vehicle: Twenty-seven-foot Fleetwood Jamboree RV with trailer, satellite dish, TV, microwave.

Education: Psychology BA, Chico State.

Occupation: Industrial nut 'n' bolt broker.

Goal: Record-setting two-hundred-mile round-trip glide on Big Sur coast.

Perfect Date: Tandem glide with spouse at Glendale air show.

Worst Fear: Becoming first quadriplegic couple in local chapter of the U.S. Hang Gliding Association (USHGA).

Choosing the right equipment, flight school, and instructor can mean the difference between becoming a skilled pilot and ending up as fertilizer. The USHGA has loads of guidelines for instructors and manufacturers. The pilot rating system is simple:

- Hang I, known informally as Fractured Ankle Level, allows pilots to skim along the ground and slam into stuff face first.

- Hang II, Shattered Pelvis Level, involves making smooth S-turns into large stationary objects such as telephone poles.

- At Hang III, Icarus Level, hang gliders make 360-degree turns into the path of commercial airliners.

- Hang IV, French Level, is earned by pilots who make an inverted stall, collapse their fragile craft, and attempt to deploy a parachute.

- Hang V, Master Level, is awarded posthumously.

Hang gliding, a distant cousin of sailing, offers some of the same dangers. Hang gliders, like sailboats, have many parts that can crack, tear, and rip. Once the equipment fails, however, sailing and hang gliding seem very different. When sailors lose their boats, they have to swim. When hang gliders lose their craft, they have to sprout wings and fly.

Because weight is a crucial element of hang gliders, they must contain light, confidence-sapping materials like aluminum, nylon, and other plastics. New space-age materials like carbon fibers are making gliders even lighter and more thrilling; carbon fibers are comparatively brittle and tend to splinter imperceptibly for no particular reason.

Unlike many other sports, hang gliding becomes riskier as a practitioner's skills improve. Instead of skimming down a dune into a mere puff of a breeze as a beginner would, an expert might launch in a tailwind from an enormous diving board, known as a "ramp," installed on a cliff above a poor runway, such as a forest, which may feature something known as "ground suck."[50]

Where cliffs are unavailable, gliders can be towed into the air by a truck or boat, overshoot the truck or boat, and, still tethered, launch straight down into the tarmac.

Pilots who reach higher altitudes sometimes experience the only thing worse than ground suck: cloud suck. A thermal turns bad and launches gliders into a cloud, flips them like confetti, chews them up, and spits them out for a little ground suck.

In case of such an emergency, many hang gliders now deploy one or more parachutes, which instantly wrap around the tumbling craft in preparation for crashing. In some cases the parachute shrouds succeed in wrapping firmly around the pilot's neck, kindly rendering the person unconscious or dead before impact.

Unfortunately, many people find it impossible even to reach a rip cord during an uncontrolled fall because of mighty G forces, tangled wires, confusion, and terror.

Unlike sailing, hang gliding often appeals to the sort of show-off who feels compelled to do rolls

---

[50]A phrase traditionally inscribed on pilots' tombstones.

and dives until the wings burst or the glider stalls, goes into a spin, and, crashing to the ground, takes on the aspect of a squashed mayfly rather than a mighty eagle.

When it comes to impressing someone, few pur-

CARNAL SOARING

ARCHETYPE PROFILE: ACE GLIDER PILOT

Appearance: Military bearing, slight paunch, aviator shades.

Home: Ft. Collins, Colorado.

House: Spacious, immaculate ranch house.

Education: Flying 28 Vietnam combat missions off the aircraft carrier *Kitty Hawk.*

Favorite Clothing: Brooks Brothers slacks, button-down shirt, boat shoes.

Occupation: Bank president.

Vehicles: Jaguar XJS, Toyota 4-Runner with trailer for glider.

Goal: Retire a multimillionaire at fifty-five.

Worst Fear: Another real estate collapse.

suits are more effective than a silent pirouette among the clouds in your very own sailplane. Unfortunately, due to the single-seat configuration of most sailplane cockpits, fondling anyone but yourself will be impossible during the flight. But as the object of your desire hangs around near the runway, looking skyward at your plane as it swoops like a giant white plastic bird, you may very well score valuable romantic points.

Some sailplanes have two or three seats, of course, and these are sought after by glider pilots the world over. Compared to flying a "private plane," soaring seems like a fine art. Soaring usually does require getting towed into the air behind a "private plane," but once the cord connecting the two is released, the glider soars into the sunshine without any sounds except the wind and the gentle moaning of the airsick passenger.

The FAA requires glider pilots to have licenses, but less training is required to pilot a glider than a motorized plane[51]—only about forty hours. Sailplanes also cost much less than Cessnas. With practice, talent, and the right weather conditions, a glider pilot can ride thermals and fly for hundreds of miles before landing and looking for a bus depot.

For under $2000 you can solo in two weeks and get your pilot's license with seven hours of solo flying, plus written and in-flight tests. Breaking your neck takes another half a second.

Like a great bird of prey or an albatross, you

---

[51]Without gasoline on board, a falling glider poses a much smaller threat to innocent people on the ground.

SUAVE-MATIC QUICK REFERENCE GUIDE: AIR SPEAK

STATEMENT	MEANING
I was riding a ridge up through twelve thousand feet when I passed the critical angle of attack and went into a stall.	The tracks were too steep for my roller coaster, and I started to roll backward.
My left wing dropped, and the nose started yawing to the left.	Because the tracks were made of air, my fiberglass train immediately headed for a destination of its own choosing.
I applied the right rudder, but perhaps a bit too hard, and as the glider weather-vaned it began to roll.	Air meeting the side of the fuselage and vertical fin turned the craft like a weather vane while it spun like an arrow.
I had entered an unexplored flight situation.	I had not been trained to handle this kind of crisis without blind panic.

STATEMENT	MEANING
As it went into a spin, the craft began to descend vertically.	The craft began to fall like a large leaf.
I opened my FAA *Pilot's Operating Handbook* and turned to the section on spin recovery.	It was difficult to read my manual with my head hammering against the plexiglass cowl/aluminum struts.
I learned that slow and overly cautious control movements must be avoided during spin recovery.	It turned out that a certain level of panic is OK.
As per instructions, I applied full opposite rudder in a brisk manner and then brisk positive straightforward movement of the elevator control.	I made a very hard right turn and dived with my guts all twisted around inside.
I was pleased not to induce an excessive and unfavorable yawing effect with my rudder.	Luckily I didn't push it so far that I started spinning in the opposite direction.
It's good to be standing on deck again.	I thought I'd be with Jimmy Hoffa by now.

will seek lift from three sources: columns of warm air, such as those rising from freshly plowed fields, wind sliding up mountainsides, and wind waves "bouncing" off the ground on the lee side of mountains. The best pilots have a sixth sense, a "bird brain," that allows them to guess where the air is rising quickly and smoothly.

NAME-DROPPER'S NOTE: WESTERN NEVADA

Waves of air in the Minden area of western Nevada, just east of Lake Tahoe, provide some of the best soaring anywhere. Waves forming in the lee of the Sierra Nevada can lift a sailplane *half a mile per second* and regularly rocket planes up to 25,000 feet.

With glide ratios in the range of forty to one, high-performance gliders regularly travel hundreds of miles in a flight; a few have soared more than a thousand miles on a single flight.

Like every other aerial sport, the hard part of soaring is stopping. The glider pilot is at a severe disadvantage without a motor. If the sailplane gets below the correct glide path, for example, the pilot may not be able to get back up onto it in time to reach the runway. "Go-arounds," second attempts to land, are not always available to a glider pilot.

Naturally, your life and health insurance agents will be interested to know that you've taken up soaring. Be sure to ask them for a refund of any premiums paid after your policies have been canceled.

How to Make Your Heroic Deeds Sound Plausible

Most people are ignorant enough not to be impressed by the average heroic deed. A friend of ours told his grandmother he planned to climb Mount McKinley. "Don't people *drive* up it?" she asked. "Isn't there a *hotel* at the top?"

Talking about your superhuman strength or how you face death with pleasure will turn off most potential devotees and may result in humiliation. If people ask about your adventures, do not speak of the hardships you have borne or the dangers you have relished. Rather than trying to regale a reluctant audience with your mighty deeds, have someone else do it for you, keep everything to yourself, or use one of these methods:

THE "I AM SUCH AN IDIOT" GAMBIT

Example: What a fool you were to windsurf from Miami to Rio. "I didn't look real closely at the map—it turns out Rio is a lot farther south than I figured. Plus—get this—they don't even speak Spanish in Brazil. And the vendors wouldn't take dollars when I got to Ipanema and wanted a cold soda. Can you believe that?"

THE "I DON'T TALK ABOUT THAT ANYMORE" APPROACH

Make dark allusions to tragedy and ugly emotional scar tissue.

"Why did I give up that sport? Let's just say I don't enjoy bagging body parts all that much."

JUST THE FACTS: A HIGH FAILURE/CASUALTY RATE

"We started with nine canoes. By noon we were down to three."

"Fourteen people went for the top that season. Only two of us made it. Only five came home. With a grand total of eighty-six fingers and toes."

IMPLYING YOUR COURAGE AND SKILL WITH OPF: OTHER PEOPLE'S FEAR

"These two *National Geographic* photographers saw the first set of rapids and decided they'd walk home."

"You should've seen the guys jump when I walked into camp carrying this big fat pit viper."

"This surgeon we'd brought along went wild when I said I was going to go for the summit. She acted like a bleeding abrasion, a separated shoulder, and a few broken ribs were worth getting excited about. She says, 'You need a medi-vac helicopter.' I say, 'No, Doc, I need a tube of Neosporin and an immediate improvement in your attitude.' "

Index